Making a Life

MAKING A LIFE

Things That Matter and How We Create Them

SARAH AUSTIN CASSON

Book Design by Sarah Lahay

First Edition 2026

ISBN: 979-8-9944823-1-5 (ebook)
ISBN: 979-8-9944823-0-8 (paperback)

Library of Congress Control Number: 2026901487

Published by Dair Press
Berkeley, California & Copenhagen, Denmark
www.DairPress.com

Dair Press
A publishing company founded on intellectual curiosity and a sense of adventure.

For Finn,
my delightful goofball

Contents

Introduction

I first picked up knitting needles in 2019 when I visited Denmark. As I walked around Copenhagen, it seemed like every Danish woman could knit, and was currently doing so. Mostly in their twenties and thirties, they sat in groups and pairs. Sometimes men were part of these groups, but without yarn in their hands. Often a nearby stroller or two held a content kiddo, breathing in the fresh air. Cafes were full of these hip, attractive ladies. So were parks and buses—and the airport gates.

Before that trip to Denmark, I figured that knitting was an impossible skill no reasonable person could learn. Sure, maybe grandmothers who had been stuck in 1950s domesticity could do it, but I figured no one of my generation—nor any reasonable person with a deep desire not to be confined by gender norms—could knit, much less actually create something worth wearing.

I couldn't stop staring at these women in their stylish boatneck striped sweaters and delicate scarves. They were laughing and chatting as their hands moved with yarn and needles.

I was surprised how much I wanted that—the sweaters, the ongoing creative activities, the laughing with friends at a cafe devoid of laptops. Looking around Copenhagen, I figured that maybe I had been wrong about knitting's style and demographic. I realized that, hey, if they *all* could do it, why couldn't I?

So on that trip, I signed up for an "Introduction to Knitting" class at Tante Grøn CPH, a knitting shop in the heart of Copenhagen. For two hours the owner, Susanne Toft, showed me the knit and purl stitches. I spent the rest of my trip carrying around a handful of teal yarn and my printed instructions, endlessly knitting a lopsided tea towel.

I never thought picking up knitting needles would lead me to think about feminism, creativity, or the joys of impracticality. Honestly, I figured I'd get a few sweaters out of it. I certainly didn't think it would lead me down a path of asking what was missing from my life.

I should have known better. My lesson with Susanne was my first hint that creative activities can offer not just instruction but also community, mentorship, and friendship. It offered, so to speak, the whole ball of yarn: playing with the math of stitch counting, algebra and geometry, interesting conversations, beautiful colors, complex environmental issues, historical significance, avenues for exploring what womanhood means, and playful ways to express myself.

I am a scientist—an environmental anthropologist, to be more specific. For over a decade, I've spent my time traveling from project to project in remote parts of the world, consulting on conservation strategies, and cranking out interdisciplinary papers on conservation and climate change. Do you need an in-depth paper on conserving wilderness that includes research, stats, biology, and social science? I'm your gal.

Need a beautiful drawing or music composition? Maybe ask someone else. I never really meshed with the arts—though I come from a family of craftspeople who can seemingly make and draw just about anything. I swear there isn't an art practice my sister hasn't just naturally picked up on her first try. Numbers, facts, abstract philosophies: that's where I have always felt most comfortable.

Creative stuff always seemed to be things other people did. Not me. I think a lot of us can feel that way sometimes. We go to a modern art museum and joke that we could do the Jackson Pollock paintings. Sure, maybe we kinda could— but not really. No way could most of us replicate his classical, technical drawings (or those of his wife, Lee Krasner, an equally talented abstract expressionist painter).

Does that mean we're not creative? I used to think so. Now, I'm not so sure. I realized I needed a bigger definition of creativity—one that didn't require me to produce museum-worthy pieces. Figuring that out took me a while.

After that trip to Denmark, I kept knitting. Mostly as a practical thing: It gets surprisingly cold in the evenings in California where my partner, Sam, and I were living at the time. I wanted sweaters that fit me, and a hand-knit sweater can sell for hundreds of dollars. I figured I surely could make myself one.

I purchased my first pattern in February 2020 and knit through the height of the pandemic, turning out a plethora of sweaters, each one slowly better than the last. I didn't make bread or do TikTok dances. I knit. I watched (and rewatched) YouTube tutorials on specific knot techniques. I made lots of mistakes. I knit a chunk of one sweater inside out before I understood what I was doing. It felt like too much effort to undo those rows of stitches and so I left the mistake, carrying on with the sweater.

I went from not great to honestly pretty good at knitting. It felt lovely to dip into the slow consistency of building something while everything around me disintegrated. It was immensely more enjoyable to play with colors and new techniques than my usual activities: manically refreshing news sites and digging into reports on accelerating case numbers.

I don't think it's a coincidence that during such a hard time, I instinctively reached for something tangible, slow, soft, and creative. Most of us did this during those years.

And yet, it still didn't occur to me that knitting represented something that was missing from my life. That I needed or wanted useful creativity for its own sake. I still saw it as a practical task.

What would I define as creative? I realized that for me it meant something useful, something meditative. It meant making something or doing something—and that something didn't need to result in an original object. It could just bring me joy.

I asked myself: What is it about my knitting that feels creative? I wasn't designing the pattern, dyeing the yarn, or anything like that. It certainly felt creative—in the same way making a homemade meal does. Following a pattern is like cooking from a recipe. How closely you follow it and how advanced the techniques are depends on your skills. But you're still following someone else's instructions.

The first sweaters I made were slightly more colorful versions of a Duncan Hines cake: add eggs, oil, and water, stir and bake. Frost however you like, and eat your delicious creation. That same process will give you a basic sweater. You only need to know how to knit and purl—and buy a good pattern.

As you gain skill (and confidence), you can take that cake mix to the next level. My mom used to make me a 3D bear cake for my birthdays when I was little. The batter was the same—my favorite, Double Chocolate Duncan Hines—but the outcome was wildly different. She'd use food dye to get the brown fur icing just right, using a special decorating tip to pipe the frosting to give the fur some texture. The bear might get a pink dress or blue overalls. Maybe even a bow.

Clearly, my mom's cake making was a creative process.

So what does that creativity mean? Looking at my knitting, I think it means using your imagination, thinking widely (and perhaps a bit weirdly). It can mean crafting something from where there was nothing—and putting your own spin on it. It can also mean how you make decisions, selecting one thing over another.

There's a recent book, *Unraveling*, in which the author, journalist Peggy Orenstein, crafts each step of her sweater's existence: She shears a sheep, spins the wool into yarn, and dyes that yarn—all before knitting it into what she describes as "the world's ugliest sweater." Orenstein never claims that her way of approaching a sweater is the only way to make it creative. Infusing each step with another layer of creativity, her process is a cool way to look at knitting.

Even without making my own yarn, I realized my sweater making can be a creative process: what colors and patterns I pick, the physical act of the knitting stitch movements, learning new skills, particular stylistic decisions

I make along the way, and many other things. After a while, you know enough to see something in the instructions and decide to employ a different technique for ease, appearance, tools available, or whatever.

I am not designing sweaters when I make one. The designers whose patterns I follow aren't creating the concept of a sweater for the first time. They're iterating on what has come before.

Which is all to say that creativity isn't as restrictive as I think most of us make it out to be. I don't know if it's only restricted to the act of making itself. Making something is an obvious application of creativity—and surely a very visual, tangible example. But it isn't the only form of creativity. We're creative when we think from a new perspective, approach a problem differently, and reexamine what counts as food or not. It's when we use our imagination. That, luckily, is only as limited as we let it be. We craft our things and our lives.

One of the words that comes up quickly when engaging in any sort of creativity is the word *craft*. It's been crazily overused. There's probably a craft version of anything you can think of: craft beer, craft furniture, craft soap, craft clothes, craft juice, craft sandwiches, wild crafted sea moss . . . it goes on and on. It's a term that's been stale for at least a decade now.

These days, craft *anything* more often elicits an eye roll than a second look.

There's a reason the term gets used. People want to take care in making things—and if they're selling it, they want you to know about that care.

We want to know about that care, too. We pay extra for the hope that our organic food (or cotton mattress) was made lovingly—and with kindness to those who made it. We support small businesses to keep our communities flourishing and put our finances where our politics align. We ache for a world of connectedness, kindness, community, respect, and care—for our loved ones and strangers alike.

Creativity is common. It's ancient. It can be deeply impractical in fun ways. Sure, we like to think those Paleolithic cave paintings were very practical art—a record of a hunt, a lesson for future hunts, a storytelling device to pass on essential myths. Maybe they were. They might have also resulted from someone wanting to put something beautiful somewhere.

Creativity, in a good way, feels like an indulgence to me. Not like a chocolate cake. But like a healthy, well-cooked, lovingly made meal. It's something we all should give ourselves more often.

My background as an anthropologist means that when I first started asking questions about creative traditions, I immediately thought about different countries and cultures. I wanted to know how hotspots of these traditions came about and why they still foster such creative women.

I didn't want just to be an observing academic—I wanted to replicate for myself what these cultures of tradition had fostered: creative communities, mentorship, and the intentionality that comes from valuing the physical things we choose to create beyond their price tag.

I wanted to delve into these things the same way Matthew Crawford explores the deep value of pursuing manual trades in *Shop Class as Soulcraft* and Robert Pirsig questions what actually matters in *Zen and the Art of Motorcycle Maintenance*. I wanted my own inquiries to reflect that I'm not a middle-aged dude. I'm a millennial woman—and I don't give a shit about motorcycles.

My partner and I are both travelers. My conservation work often involves chunks of time in different countries. Sam, who shares my wanderlust, can often work from wherever we are. After the height of the pandemic, we landed in different spots around the world. I started immersing myself in creativity skills and learning from women doing them.

I could have chosen from a multitude of creative practices. But, given where we were traveling, I picked traditions that fit with my specific interests: knitters in Denmark; sea foragers in Mie Prefecture, Japan; and practitioners of traditional sewing arts in Kyoto. Could I have instead included Irish lacework or something else? Sure. But lace isn't my jam (sorry, Irish ancestors), and I wanted to add a level of practicality to my deeply impractical venture.

I didn't want to make for the purpose of creating whatever. The journey matters, but so does the destination. I wanted to deeply indulge in creativity and then walk away with items I would eat, wear, or *do* something with. To have a semblance of balance between creating for the sake of play and thinking about the end result. If lace is your thing (or literally anything else), that would count as a good balance for you.

I knew I wanted to keep knitting, of course. But I'm an active person. I like moving my body. I wanted some practices that got my body in motion.

I found two more creative activities that require your whole body. The first was sewing. The actual stitching part, it turns out, is only a small part of sewing. Beyond washing and drying the material, there's the ironing, the tracing of the design, the cutting of fabric, and so many more steps.

The second, sea foraging, might sound a bit niche. But, as I found out, gathering food from the sea is as big of a deal as looking for mushrooms in the forest. People walk the tide pools and dive the near shore in search of seaweed and shellfish. I wanted to go to the source, the traditional sea-foraging women of Japan—the ama.

Up through their eighties, the ama dive into the ocean, down dozens of feet, and have been doing it for thousands of years, with the how-to passed from grandmother to mother to daughter. Sea foraging doesn't seem like the most obvious creative practice. After all, it isn't making things. But, as I'd learn, it turns out looking at how the ama sea forage helps expand our definition of craft into something bigger and embodied.

So that's what I did: sew, sea forage, and knit. With each of these creative activities, I made sure to find women to learn from who excelled in each tradition. I met with a woman in Kyoto revitalizing and modernizing an ancient sewing tradition. Off the coast of Mie Prefecture in southeast Japan, I dove and talked with the ama about their sea foraging. And I met with Danish knitwear designers who, through their mega Instagram accounts, have quite profitable full-time jobs selling PDF patterns of sweaters.

I then went back to the United States to see where I could do these creative activities and find community and mentorship at home. I learned that many of my longtime friends there were also starting to play in these creative activities. With old friends and new, I went seaweed collecting, learned how to fish with old-school techniques, dipped into tidal nature journaling. We talked knitting, hung out in cafes and parks knitting together and discussing patterns. Sewed our clothing and wore them out to fancy dinners and outdoor adventures.

I ended up with the Danish cafe scenes I had been so jealous of—friends hanging out, doing something creative, no phones in sight, and a lot of loud laughter.

So yeah, this is a book about a millennial woman making her clothes and foraging food, edging uncomfortably close to a laughable stereotype. It's also about these bigger things: what it means to make things in a world of cheap e-commerce, to take the inefficient route, to play with physical objects, to learn from people doing exciting things with their lives, to look at the roles material things play in connecting us in a world that can so often feel disconnected. Basically, I wanted to make something out of seemingly nothing.

At least that's what this book *was* about. All of this was amplified by what I started to create halfway through this journey: a baby. When Sam and I found out about this new life growing inside of me, I began to radically rethink my own life and what the concept of making a life means.

Pregnancy became this larger metaphor for me (as I, too, became larger). Almost all the experts I met in creative traditions around the world were mothers. Mothers who enjoyed their lives, their creativity, and their children. Being pregnant as I foraged, knit, and did sewing projects in the Bay Area forced me to be more creative about what I made—and humbled me in new ways, as my energy went mostly to creating a tiny human.

It brought me deeper into these traditions and communities. The women I met had things to teach me about knitting techniques, yes, but also about motherhood—and how one finds the space to joyfully go after all the things. Even in places where mothers often get told they need to sacrifice in order to be good, to be practical, to be responsible.

I have never been very good at being practical. To my relief, it seemed that neither were these women. They dreamed big and went after those dreams. They dove into deep oceans, brought ancient sewing techniques into modern designs, and made global companies out of their love of pretty yarn—all while drawing on lineages of women who have done the same thing.

Pregnancy, I realized, is not much different than other projects millennial women are pursuing to bring useful creativity, intentionality, and community into their lives. It is slowly creating bones and eyeballs—and hopefully a spunky, somewhat annoyingly independent spirit. Since time immemorial, this has been the original definition of women's work. Of doing the creating that keeps our species able to continue the lineage of wonder at our brief existence, as something instead of nothing. We exist because women create.

After all, what does it mean to create something—be it a human or a sweater?

Part I

Learning

Chapter 1

Red Sock

On a July day in 2022, I found myself swinging in a hammock in the Amazonian jungle knitting a red sock.

I was in the Brazilian wilderness for a conservation project. After the height of the pandemic, I had gotten back to my life of projects and traveling. I—like an idiot—brought my knitting. Because what else are you going to do in a jungle but knit wool?

On a midday break, I hid in the shade of my hut, lying in my hammock under my mosquito net in only a bra and underwear as sweat dripped off me onto the roughly hewn planks of wood, full of splinter potential. I put in earplugs to block out the sound of termites speedily destroying this newly built hut (nothing lasts too long in a jungle). I figured I'd lie there, relax somehow, and knit a bit.

The jungle, it turns out—as probably any reasonable person can tell you—is not an ideal place to knit, even something as thin and small as a sock. I couldn't bear to hold the yarn. The red wool felt sticky in my hands and made me feel even hotter.

There was no practical reason to be knitting. I was attempting to knit as a way for me to *not* think about the scorpion that had just fallen from my hut's ceiling or the poisonous snake I'd seen in the river where I bathed. I did not need a single red sock. I had plenty of socks. I always overpack socks.

And yet, I felt incredibly annoyed that I couldn't knit—and hadn't brought anything similar to play with. Knitting, for me, had unknowingly become play. After maybe the third sweater (I mean, how many sweaters does one need? Two, probably . . .), knitting had secretly switched from practical to fun.

It turned out that I got angsty without that creative play I had gotten so used to during those long days of pandemic lockdowns. Not angsty enough to actually knit the sock—it immediately got tucked back into a ziplock bag and not touched until I returned to California—but angsty nonetheless.

As I crankily tried to figure out something else to do with myself during the heat of the days in the jungle, I realized that creativity, on a deeper level, might be missing from my life.

After two years of COVID restrictions, my partner, Sam, and I were ready to go somewhere other than the 300-square-foot apartment we'd been renting in Los Angeles—and do something that utterly did not involve screens. Like a lot of people, we were pent up and wanting to travel.

After I returned from the Amazon, we did a quick weeklong turnaround of laundry, packing, and logistics before boarding a flight for an open-ended exploration of what would come next. This was in 2022, so countries were still slowly opening back up to foreigners. We couldn't plan that far in advance, even if we wanted to.

The plan was to head to Indonesia, a place I'd worked often, for a few months. We then continued onward to southern Japan to enroll in language school and eat all the things we love: katsu, ramen, yakitori, donburi, sushi, gyoza.

Before you close this book being like, *What is this lady doing with her life?* hear me out. My work brings me to locations where people often have very different ways of life than most Americans. It reminds me that there isn't just one way to make a life.

I get pretty bad jet lag—and hate being tired—so I like to plan long, slow trips. I'm talking months, not days.

I situate myself somewhere and get to sink into the place. I find a favorite coffee shop, get to know some familiar faces, and run for exercise and exploration. Since strong Wi-Fi now exists in most places, computer work can happen with a bit of thought to time zones and time management.

When asked about my ability to travel to these remote places, I often give the same passive answer: My work brings me to places around the world. But that's a cop-out. I'm also a try-hard who has thought deeply about the way I want to live my life. When we travel, Sam and I use the age-old budgeting advice: Prioritize and indulge in what you want while ruthlessly cutting everything else.

You pay for travel in two ways—time or money (or both, if that's the type of trip you're looking for). What people often don't realize is that when you travel for a while, you aren't traveling the same way you'd vacation. You stay in places without AC, you take public transportation, you make your own meals. Yes, you eat the sushi and drink the fancy cafe drinks, but you also eat the 7-Eleven bento boxes and drink the vending machine coffee.

I once saved $50 by taking a ten-hour overnight ferry instead of a thirty-minute plane ride to a remote island in Indonesia. Was I exhausted (having slept on a straw mat on the deck) and very much not thinking the money saved was worth it by the time I actually arrived at my destination after a sixteen-hour delay on top of the ten-hour ferry ride? Yes. Did I meet some really nice Indonesians as we shared food and small talk in the purgatory that is unknown, continuous travel delays? Also yes. When I returned to that island to go diving there again, did I take the plane? Absolutely I did. Was the diving so spectacular that it didn't really matter how I got there? Yes indeed.

When our time was over in Indonesia, we both wanted to stay in Asia. We had always wanted to spend more time in Japan. It's a large, long country packed with people and amazing nature. Its cities are dense and its forests wild. A quick google confirmed that the Japanese borders were still closed to foreigners with a few exceptions. One of the exceptions that fit us was a student visa to study the language. Our decision was easily made: We'd learn Japanese in Japan.

We decided on Fukuoka, the foodie, hipster capital of Japan. Fukuoka is somewhat like both of the Portlands in the US—where millennials go to retire. Far in the south of Japan on the island of Kyushu, it's an eight-hour ride on a bullet train ride from Tokyo and culturally worlds away from the capital's workaholism. Many Japanese millennials move from Tokyo to Fukuoka for the more relaxed lifestyle.

Fukuoka might be the coolest city in Japan. It has amazing food. Literally any restaurant you walk into will likely be delicious and family-run. It makes food in other parts of Japan seem just *fine*, which is saying something.

Everyone in Fukuoka seems active. The city is surrounded by gorgeous mountains and the ocean. Surfers and runners are in abundance. Their version of Central Park, Ohori Park, is such a popular running destination that one lane of the loop around the park's lake is paved with a rubbery track surface for the runners.

When we arrived in Japan, I still had the partially knit red sock with me. I had brought it to Indonesia from the Amazon but didn't knit in Indonesia either—the same problem continued: It was too darn hot. I packed it again as we traveled to Japan, figuring that since we were showing up in winter, I might be more amenable to knitting.

My creative itch had only grown stronger since the jungle. I knit by myself for the first few days in our Airbnb when we arrived in Japan, but found myself still wanting more creativity. I didn't know how I wanted more—or why—just that I wanted more than knitting by myself. I thought maybe knitting with others would help.

We first stayed in an Airbnb in Chuo Ward, not too far from the Tenjin subway station in one direction and Ohori Park in the other. The Tenjin area is full of shops, great restaurants, bars, cafes, and museums. Ohori Park is this luscious green splash in an otherwise concrete city. In true Japanese style, the lake used to be the moat of Fukuoka castle, the ruins of which still stand. We crammed ourselves, our dive equipment, yoga mats, and computers with our digital vocab flashcards into the small Airbnb, figuring that we'd soon get settled and excited to start exploring the city. After our visas ended, we'd figure out what to do next.

Fukuoka was chilly and only got colder as we got deeper into winter. It was a wet, rainy cold that required often having an umbrella with you. No one would rent us an apartment, a problem many foreigners run into in Japan. We settled into a tiny, awful but doable, overpriced one through a rental service that explicitly re-rents apartments to foreigners who can't get normal apartments.

Even the language learning felt hard. The school we went to was one of the more relaxed language schools in Japan, with small class sizes and kind, interested teachers. But it still needed to follow the government-mandated curriculum of Japanese language schools granting student visas. The twenty hours of weekly classroom time was coupled, I was aghast to realize, with an expectation of twenty hours of homework. The teachers expected us to memorize hundreds of words a week.

Our French and German classmates loved manga and couldn't comprehend that I didn't know anything about anime. I hoped I'd find community another way—maybe through knitting. I started googling and found the only yarn shop, Amuhibi, in the city. It's one of the few yarn shops in Japan that isn't in the major cities farther north. Tucked away down a random tiny side street, it is in a house turned into a shop among other tiny houses-turned-shops that you could completely miss without noticing their small signs.

Once you open Amuhibi's door, there's no confusion about whether you've walked into someone's living room. Yarn (mostly imported from Europe), knitting accessories, and sample knitted sweaters cover the first floor. The second floor has big, sun-filled windows, a large mural, piles of yarn ready to be brought downstairs, and big tables with chairs to accommodate about fifteen knitters.

Looking around, I had high hopes that this knitting shop would be all I needed to scratch my creative itch in Japan—a hidden knitting spot where I'd make new friends and beautiful sweaters.

I eagerly signed up for their second-floor one-hour knitting sessions, where for a few bucks you can grab a spot and just knit. I signed up a week in advance because I figured they'd sell out (who wouldn't want to knit there?!) and I wanted to make sure I grabbed my spot.

I need not have worried—when I returned for the session, no one else was there, other than two cats. One of the cats wanted to sit on my knitting and got annoyed I wanted to knit instead of petting her. The other one ran under a table and looked nervously at me.

The only time I knit upstairs there with fellow knitters was during a workshop led by the Danish designer Marianne Isager, a rock star in the knitting world who runs Isager Yarn, a company considered the gold standard for yarn and knitting patterns.

Perhaps unsurprisingly, the best patterns, yarn, and some of the most creative knitters come from Northern Europe, especially Denmark. The Japanese knitters turned out in force to work on sweaters from Marianne's new book, *A Knitting Life*.

You would have thought these women had just met Taylor Swift. When she pulled out a sweater, everyone went bananas. No one chitchatted during the entire workshop—they were hanging on to Marianne's every word. Everyone was very nice but not there to make friends.

These women were already expert knitters. What they could crank out in an afternoon's workshop was astonishing—intense knots and colorwork. They were doing the knitting equivalent of studying with a master when you're already an expert.

That was not me. I wanted to bumble around with knitting and make myself something stylish with others doing the same. There's value in doing things around others in a group, even when everyone is in their zone, not chitchatting too much. This is the way many women have been doing creative practices for eons. But I wasn't good enough at knitting to be able to do that with this group.

Until I was knitting with this group of expert knitters, I didn't realize how much I watch (and rewatch) YouTube tutorial videos to help me learn (and relearn) knitting techniques. If I'm knitting alone, it's not really a problem for me to replay the same three-minute video aloud over and over until I understand what to do. That's very much not okay around other people.

Add on top of that, everyone else was knitting from instructions in Japanese. The ladies who worked at the shop had translated mine into English using Google Translate—an extremely kind gesture. But that also meant I was working off instructions originally written in Danish, translated into English, translated in Japanese, and then translated back into English.

So sometimes I wasn't sure if it was a technique I didn't know or a translation error. When I absolutely could not find a description of a particular knot with my not-so-subtle googling, Marianne nicely told me, "Oh yeah, that's not translated right." Then she showed me how to do what the instructions were trying to convey.

When a woman sitting next to me saw me struggling with another knot technique, she put down her own knitting and politely showed me how to do it. I got it after she showed me, but ten minutes later, when I had to do the technique again, I had already forgotten how to do it. I didn't want to bother her again, so I fudged the technique and moved along, trying to ignore the somewhat large hole I had created.

It was pretty awkward to be slowly bumbling along as everyone else had already seemingly cranked out half a sweater. I'm fine being awkward—how else do you learn? If it had been that type of environment every knitting session, that probably would have been fine with me. A bit intense but doable. But other than that one workshop, I never saw anyone else when I knit upstairs.

I mean, I was knitting. Wasn't that what I wanted? To just knit the damn sock? But I still didn't feel creatively fulfilled.

I can knit by myself anywhere. I was looking for the other parts that come with a creative practice—the friends, the learning, the chatting about different projects, the fun of doing similar things with other people.

Still, I kept showing up every week. I'd knit, play with the cat, and stare out the window at the drizzling rain.

Maybe, I thought, I wasn't ready for a creative community yet. I needed to do some basic thinking on what it was about creativity and a creative practice appealed to me.

Obviously people have been making these things for thousands of years. There weren't stores in the caves. Between then and now, we've figured out how to make bronze statues, ceramics, jewelry, and so much more. America has had a long tradition of groups focused on living with intentionality with things, nature, and other people, like vegetarians, feminists, abolitionists, the literary transcendentalist community in Massachusetts in which Louisa May Alcott grew up, and the celibate Shaker movement that made fantastic handmade minimalist furniture.

It's an act in opposition to how so many of us live our lives today. We work intensely at our paid job and then, in spare moments, try to scrap some recreation and community together. The job part gets the priority, and everything else is done quickly: fast fashion, fast food, and quick coffee dates scheduled weeks in advance.

This isn't new: Slow food has been a large international movement since the 1980s and was eventually followed by slow fashion and slow media. What seems to be bubbling up to the surface, even beyond these slow movements, is a search for a more meaningful, more creative way to make a life.

In reaction to the pandemic and the seemingly increasing chaos of the world, people are returning in surprising numbers to old ways of doing and being. They are knitting their own sweaters, foraging their dinners, and mending their jeans. Not because it is financially thrifty or practical. Usually it's the opposite.

Across America, these movements are alive and well. Folks are mending their clothes with ancient Japanese techniques. They're sewing new outfits, thinking about this season's fashions but also twenty years from now—and how particular, old-fashioned techniques might help create longevity in their shirts. They're farmers—or meeting their farmers—concerned about the animal, plant, and petroleum materials used to make our clothes. This concern influences what sweaters they knit while also nudging them toward knitting a few beloved pieces instead of online shopping every winter.

They're wearing these outfits to forage the tidal zones, while thinking about what they're gathering, how much and in what seasons. Most aren't living exclusively off the land but certainly think more critically about their food—who harvested it in what season and who prepared it—when grocery shopping and dining out. They're doing all of this out of concern for the other critters we share this planet with. Crafting, making, foraging are also just plain fun. It's impractical in a delightful way.

Many, like me, are millennials—and yes, we understand what we think we've discovered has been around forever, but we're different and have a much better way of doing something humans have always been doing. I say this tongue-in-cheek, of course. It's a movement that is radically claiming something distinctly not radical or new. What is great about these groups is that they're going after reclaiming the original meaning— of infusing their things with intentionality and thus doing so with their entire lives.

Making things, in one sense, is the most impractical thing ever. Why mend something when you can just go out and buy something shiny and new? Slowing down and doing things with our hands, caring about things enough to repair them, and wanting community beyond our office Zoom calls has exploded in recent years. We desire to do things that matter. We want to matter.

Creating something out of nothing reminds us both of our individual power and connectedness and of the fragility of our lives. Stitches can unravel. Everything was once nothing. One day, it will be nothing again.

Richard Sennett is a sociologist who has thought deeply about the process of craftsmanship. His book *The Craftsman* expands the definition of craft to everything we do. Craft, he argues, is "good work for its own sake," an approach that applies to coders as much as it does woodworkers. Done in the right way, being a salesperson, baker, or parent is craft.

Craft, as he sees it, doesn't have to result in *something*. One need not be making art bound for museums—or even art at all. And one certainly doesn't need to be living in a remote picturesque village devoid of technology, sculpting marble or whatever to approach life as a craftsman. You just need to be doing things with intention.

I wanted this type of creative practice *and*, where possible, I wanted to end up with something material that was beautiful and useful.

I like material objects. Too often, though, in our runaway consumer culture, any love of things gets reduced to materialism. I'm not sure that's always a good idea. When we think about materialism and the things we surround ourselves with, we usually cue up images of gluttony, of overflowing landfills. We literally have too many things in the world. A reaction to this recent swing against consumerism has been to get rid of things—to purge, only keeping the things that mean something to you.

What if we thought about materialism a bit more like an anthropologist? That would require considering what we *value* about our material things. It'd require examining the intentionality in the things we surround ourselves with.

Within the field of anthropology, there's a famous concept: "thinking through making." It was coined by British anthropologist Tim Ingold in his 2013 book *Making: Anthropology, Archaeology, Art and Architecture.* He uses the phrase to get at the idea that thinking doesn't only exist in books or in our heads. Thinking is also created by how we interact with the objects we surround ourselves with. The creative act of making something, he argues, is itself a way of philosophizing about the world.

What does it mean to think through making? It means interacting with our physical world in a deeper way. It requires participation in our existence. It brings our interactions and thoughts about the world out of the realm of the cerebral to the physical.

Woodworking is an oft-cited example of that: Stay too cerebral and you might cut off a finger. Peter Korn is a woodworker, writer, and teacher who has thought a lot about what it means to make physical objects (and has worked a lot with said physical objects—he's not just a dude in an office pontificating about creative practices). In his 2015 book, *Why We Make Things and Why It Matters,* he writes "In many ways, the coffee table in my living room and the desk at which I sit are like the book that you are reading. Each came into being through a creative process in which I explored ideas about life. When I am making furniture, I think with things; when I am writing, I think with words. Both methodologies are powerful tools."

Making things makes you think about things. Not just the stuff you create. Yes, you start to think about supply chains and the many hands and brains that went into the creation of the pen you're writing with—but also nonhuman creations, like rocks. Those, too, were made, albeit by geological forces over millennia. Everything was once something else and will be something else in the future. We are constantly being made and remade.

I had a lot of options for creative practices to try in Japan. The country is known as the land of craftspeople, after all. This image is a big part of their soft diplomacy but is also a truism. Japan has a relatively high per capita of craftspeople devoting their lives to their specific tradition: potters, woodworkers, sake makers, dyers, papermakers, painters. What these craftspeople produce is some of the best in the world.

That expectation was a slight hurdle I ran into—and not just in knitting. People stereotypically take their hobbies and their crafts seriously in Japan. It's not uncommon for someone to have a day job and then a singular hobby that they really dive deep into. That's just the amateurs; I'm not even talking about the professionals who make their living as craftsperson, who take their craft extremely seriously.

What about sewing, I thought? There's a huge tradition of sewing in Japan—everything from high fashion to traditional kimonos to decorative stitching.

I'd tried to learn how to sew before. Back in Los Angeles, I'd figured I'd crank out some gorgeous, flowy dresses, that they'd fit me perfectly, and that the whole thing would be cheaper and more stylish than anything I could buy at a shop. I'd just pick a pattern, follow the instructions, and the whole thing would be this happy-go-lucky three-hour venture.

It was not. After many days of sewing and many hours of watching YouTube sewing tutorials, I ended up with one dress, an ugly lilac muumuu that absolutely swallowed me.

The machine ran really fast—it zipped through an entire line of stitching before I had quite realized what was going on. (I didn't know how to slow it down until a few days in.) The line of stitching would be done, but I'd invariably have messed something up, or put pieces together upside down or backward. Undoing machine sewing is a pain in the butt. You have to rip out all the tiny little stitches with a tiny double-pronged seam ripper that hurts a lot when you accidentally stab yourself with it.

In Los Angeles that summer, I figured, let's slow down and try hand sewing clothing. I thought the slower pace would help me understand the fitting of the pattern pieces before the machine sewed it up in a blink of an eye and I'd completely gone wrong, or not straight or whatever.

Hand sewing a shirt turned out even worse than the stupid lilac dress—and took a lot longer. For this hand-sewn shirt, I bought a kit that had all the materials you need, including the fabric pieces already cut to your size, the thread, the needles, and the pattern instructions. It seemed foolproof.

Hand sewing let me go at a slow pace. I could follow the instructions and actually execute them, unlike the machine sewing. The shirt was the size I had picked, but it was huge on me. Worse yet, my hand sewing looked like a fourth-grader had done it. Which was the last time I had sewn when I had made a quilt with my mom for Girl Scouts.

I gave up sewing. But now, in Japan, I started to think about approaching it again. I wondered: Maybe I needed a sewing creative practice even more scaled back? Something that would let me do the act of sewing without the immense pressure of caring what the finished product looked like on my body. I couldn't machine sew clothing yet. I couldn't even hand sew clothing yet. Too many moving pieces. I decided to start with a single stitch, the running stitch.

Luckily, I could choose from a plethora of ancient sewing traditions in Japan—everything from hand-making kimonos to mending old clothes. Sashiko, a type of decorative embroidery, lay somewhere in the middle, both functional and decorative. It's an old northern Japanese tradition of tiny, repetitive stitches in geometric patterns to thicken cloth for cold winters and revitalize thinning, worn-out fabric. Today, people mostly use sashiko for the decorative part—embroidering kitchen towels, blankets, or clothing with geometric waves and flowers.

Best of all for me, it only uses a running stitch to produce the many different designs. Sashiko stitches slowly build into something larger. It's literally just the running stitch over and over. It can be slightly more complicated than that, but not really.

The word *sashiko* translates to "little stabs," which is a great way of thinking about sewing. You take a piece of fabric, some thread, and a needle and then stab the fabric a bunch to get your sewing done. Good enough, move along. Thinking about sashiko this way also nicely reflects the utilitarian history of the creative practice: You can imagine a woman back in the day, being like, oh this dress, blanket, whatever is getting thin, I've gotta thicken it up—I'll stab it a bunch of times, make it pretty with some geometric design, and call it a day.

That's my type of approach to a creative practice. I can't be bothered to be a perfectionist about it. I admire the work of people who can, but I just don't have the temperament.

I had my next creative practice picked out. I just needed to find someone to teach me how to do it.

Chapter 2

Revitalization

From the outside, it can seem like almost everyone in Japan is a highly specialized craftsperson cranking out amazing art or food. The country does produce some of the best physical objects in the world. Pick a category, and there's probably someone perfecting it in Japan.

I knew, obviously, that not every person in Japan was making incredible crafts or food. I figured enough people were doing so that every city would have its share of craftspeople. It turns out that while Fukuoka is an amazing food and sport city, it's not really a craft city.

There's some crafting to be found in Fukuoka. Just not sashiko. There was the Amuhibi knitting store, of course. I found some good big-box crafting stores and, surprisingly, a few stores selling only intricate buttons, but sashiko supplies—the needles, the fabric, the thread—were in short supply. Even more scarce were teachers. I couldn't find anyone within a reasonable commute who taught sashiko.

I started looking farther afield within Japan and paying closer attention to the advertised flavors of the country's big cities. Tokyo is work. Fukuoka, food. Osaka, partying. Kyoto, craftsmanship.

I had ignored Kyoto as the most obvious place to find craft in Japan because the last time I was there I absolutely hated it. It was August 2017, sweltering hot, and overrun with tourist groups. You can find amazing museums, shrines, and torii gates all over Japan—without the crushing crowds. Yes, Kyoto has beautiful places, but it's hard to appreciate them when all you can see is other foreigners also trying to do the same.

What I didn't know—and didn't notice—on that last visit to Kyoto was the crafts. I'd missed most of what makes Kyoto special. I hadn't started knitting yet, and I still thought of creativity as something for other people, not me.

Kyoto is one of the oldest crafts cities in the world. It's only relatively recently in Japanese history that the political capital and emperor's residence are in Tokyo. For over a thousand years, both were in Kyoto.

As often happens in history, political power and wealth supported a host of Japanese crafts. Absurd levels of power and money wanted art to admire and to show off, giving us flower arranging, tea ceremonies, and ornate lacquerware.

In Kyoto today, these traditional crafts are being re-invigorated. Best of all, for my sashiko search, the crafts being modernized here aren't all tailored to the rich. Yes, you can still find amazingly skilled craftspeople weaving silk for bespoke kimonos. You can also find those continuing the sewing traditions of the other classes, techniques like sashiko and boro that were historically done to extend the life of clothing. Now they have found new life as an artistic and mindfulness practice that decorates textiles around the world—and mends a few pairs of pants from Japan to Brooklyn.

The revitalization of such sewing practices reaches beyond those that sew. It allows for the continuation of other related traditions, like the family-run Itoroku thread company that was founded in 1870, the Sanjo-Honke Misuyabari handmade needle shop that's been run by a single family since 1619, and all the many other related artisans. Do they practice a carefully guarded artistic craft that has been handed down for many generations? Yes. Do they also all have Instagram and smartphones? Of course.

While I couldn't exactly commute to Kyoto from my apartment in Fukuoka, I could search online to see if there were any interesting craftspeople there who taught sashiko. That's how I found Kazue Yoshikawa and her Instagram (@sashiko.lab).

Kazue is from southern Japan originally and moved to Kyoto for university to study art. In English class she fell in love with a fellow student, now her husband, with whom she has two kids. When they moved to New Zealand together for her husband's master's degree, she felt a bit lost as a new mother in a foreign place. So she started teaching Japanese crafts at the local community center.

Those classes quickly became focused on sashiko. When she and her family moved back to Kyoto, Kazue continued teaching foreigners how to stitch sashiko. It had become a small, bustling business right as the pandemic hit, immediately drying up her tourist customer base. Kazue pivoted again and figured out how to host her classes online.

She continued those online classes even as the borders were starting to reopen. Which is how I found myself signed up to study an ancient Japanese craft in Japan on Zoom—and be delighted by that.

The way Kazue runs her online sashiko stitching classes is the best of both worlds, even if it is still mediated by those annoying screens I'd been hoping to avoid. It's a combo of "in-person" learning and a YouTube tutorial.

First, for each class—usually weekly over a set period, like a month—Kazue hosts a live Zoom session, a combination of learning, hanging out, and stitching together. The dual camera that became popular during the pandemic really helps. One lens is focused on her hands, showing the details of each stitch, and the other on her face, giving the illusion of almost being in person. Kazue will explain a technique, ask how everyone's day is going, and talk about her own, all while all thirty of us are stitching together.

Second, and the part that helps me most: She sends out the full video afterward, small talk and all. That means you can replay the key tutorial sections as often as you want. If you can't join it live, you can just watch the recording in its entirety.

Kazue's students are from all over the world: Australia, California, India. Over the years, I've joined plenty of work calls where people are dialing in from different time zones. There's no magic time; someone always gets stuck waking up too early or staying up too late. Multicountry Zoom scheduling is often a game of chicken and politeness.

Kazue's solution is smart. She rotates class times to ensure each time zone gets at least one decently timed class during the month. One week might be 3 p.m., the next 10 a.m., and then 9 p.m. after that. For those of us in Japan, it was fairly easy. But even students who lost the time-zone lottery that week still often showed up—getting up at 4 a.m. or staying awake until 11 p.m. to join.

These weren't twenty-somethings who can pull an all-nighter and somehow be chirpy the next morning (a skill I didn't have then or now). As in most online creative classes, the demographic skewed older. In the Zoom, I was one of the few women—and we were mostly women—without white hair or grandkids.

Kazue would explain a technique, and then we'd all try it together. As we stitched, people would swap tips. Someone would ask: *What's the best pens to mark a pattern on lighter fabric?* Another would answer: *The erasable FriXion pens. You can iron them away.* Another would pipe up: *Yeah, and you can get them at Target.* Someone else: *Or Amazon!*

Or someone (cough cough, me) would get confused after a few minutes of stitching and need Kazue to explain it again. *How is it you hide the thread between the layers of fabric again?* Kazue would pause her own stitching and demonstrate it, usually with a helpful reassurance that mostly it is just a hand feel that gets easier with time. More-experienced students would chime in: *Yeah! I had such a hard time with that when I began, too.*

The first project I did with Kazue's online classes was something she called a "Coffee Fukin." Yeah, you read that right.

While Japan seemingly hates swearing, it doesn't seem to care too much about things that certainly look and sound an awful lot like English swear words. Fukuoka is shortened to FUK by everyone, pronounced *fuhk* or spelled out F-U-K. FUK COFFEE is a popular (and unironically named) cafe chain. FUK LAB 801 is a place where you can paint your own keychain and other tchotchkes. The airport code is FUK.

The "fukin" of Kazue's project refers to the name for the popular *hanafukin* sashiko projects of today. *Hana* translates to "flower" and *fukin* to "cloth." So: flower cloth. They're usually two-ply, one-by-one-foot kitchen towels embroidered with geometric sashiko designs. Many are flowers, but some feature other nature motifs, like the autumn breeze or ocean waves. Some clearly resemble their inspirations. Others, not so much. A popular hanafukin pattern is *kakinohana*, which supposedly looks like persimmon flowers—if you've been told it does and you're really looking to be agreeable.

The sashiko pattern emerges from the rhythm of horizontal, vertical, and sometimes diagonal running stitches. If you're an expert, you just know where to stitch, how often to stitch, and how long to make your stitches. If you're a beginner or someone looking to make sure your final product looks super crisp, you cheat. You use a gridded piece of fabric or a pen as a guide. It's the stitching equivalent of painting by numbers.

The creativity, then, comes from the colors and textures you choose. Yes, you might be replicating an ancient pattern done a million times by many hands. You might be using grids to keep things tidy. But at least you've customized part of it to your own aesthetics—and actually stitched all those tiny stitches.

Stitching over Zoom gave the feeling of being together, but it wasn't actually being together. As we learned during the pandemic, virtual just isn't the same as in-person. Conversations on Zoom tend to be between two people while everyone else just listens.

In person, you can form smaller groups. Have side conversations. Talk without an audience of twenty-eight others casually listening in. Speak freely without the moment being recorded and sent out for rewatching later.

As Japan started to open up, Kazue began offering a few in-person classes again. It wasn't going to be something I could do regularly—Kyoto is a two-hour, twenty-one-minute $160 one-way bullet train on the Tokaido-Sanyo Shinkansen line from Fukuoka. Nonetheless, I told my language school I'd be gone for a few days and got on a train to Kyoto.

Plus, I'll take any excuse to ride a Shinkansen. I love how fast they go. How you get to sit in a comfortable seat and watch the beautiful Japanese countryside whip by. I love the feeling of adventure and coziness inherent in a train ride.

I brought my sashiko on the Shinkansen with me. In between eating my 7-Eleven snacks and drinking the coffee from the food trolley, I stitched. A woman sitting next to me for part of the trip chatted with me about how much she also liked sashiko and wished she had brought hers.

My Japanese was too limited to have had a real conversation about why she wished that. What was it about sashiko that drew her to it?

I knew I was glad I had something to do with my hands— but the hand-feel was still hard. I can knit and stare off into space. When I tried not looking at the sashiko while stitching, I stabbed myself with the needle. That usually resulted in me loudly yelping *Ow!* in an otherwise quiet train car and stitching particularly awful stitches. I alternated between watching the countryside whip by and stitching.

As we hurtled north, the countryside slowly started looking colder and colder. The snow whipping past the window got denser. I looked down at my running sneakers (the only footwear I had with me in Japan) and wondered just how quickly they were going to be soaked through.

Minutes, it turned out. I did the penguin walk-shuffle one does on icy sidewalks and grumbled to myself. Everyone else was doing the same sloshing walk. But then I started to realize: Everyone else was just a few others. The pre-pandemic summer crowds were gone, replaced by a snowy silence.

It was calm. It was peaceful. My feet were wet, yes, but that was my own fault. I started to appreciate the thick snowflakes falling onto the curved roofs of the traditional wooden *machiya* buildings.

The snow and the continuing visa restrictions, I realized, were going to give me a glimpse into a Kyoto most imagine but never actually see. I was getting to experience Kyoto quiet, calm, and blanketed in snow so picture-perfect it looked fake.

I dropped my bags off at my *machiya* Airbnb and chatted with the woman who owned it. Seemingly everyone was chatty that day: the owner of the hip soba noodle spot where I walked right in, no waiting, to enjoy a warm lunch, the coffee roaster at a third-floor shop who took approximately forever to bring a single cup of incredibly delicious coffee, and the guy behind the counter at the 7-Eleven.

I popped into a few small shops. People smiled on the street as we made eye contact and tried not to slip in the snow. Everyone seemed to be relishing the calm brought about by the snowstorm and the slow easing of pandemic restrictions. The tourist hordes weren't back yet, but the first signs of economic recovery were showing. Kyoto's government had almost gone bankrupt during the height of the pandemic. For now, small business owners were hopeful that their shops might make it.

Everyone was so unexpectedly talkative that I almost arrived late for Kazue's in-person class. I met up with her and three other students in a new maker's space with a 3D printer, a coffee shop, and several tables for stitching or laptop work.

To get there, I'd taken modern subways and walked past extremely old historical sites, some of which are still in use today. That mix of old and new—advanced technology and ancient technique—was throughout the city. I finally understood why everyone loves Kyoto so much. Even though my feet were soggy, I was sold.

For two hours, the five of us stitched sashiko with the supplies Kazue had brought. For these shorter, one-off classes, Kazue has you do small projects so you can go home with something finished.

I picked a brown three-by-three-inch cloth square and yellow, white, and orange thread. Each student had picked different colors and different *hanafukin* patterns. Instead of demonstrating every single step for each person, Kazue had cloth tutorials of every pattern.

Most beginner-friendly sashiko patterns include three steps: horizontal stitching, vertical stitching, and diagonal stitching. On a larger piece of cloth divided into four squares, Kazue had a color-coded demo. The first three squares showed each individual step (say, just the horizontal stitching), and the fourth showed them all combined, giving you the finished look.

Stitching in-person was more fun than on Zoom. You could have a more meandering conversation. Working on a smaller project made the stitching feel more doable and less existentially endless. Getting to play with Kazue's many colorful supplies and ask her artistic opinion on what combinations might look best was genuinely fun.

At Kazue's suggestion, I tied up the corners of my finished sashiko to make my little cloth into a dish. It looked positively picturesque when I placed it on my Airbnb's wooden table. I put earrings I had just purchased at a small shop into the sashiko cloth dish and decided I liked Kyoto very much.

I met up with Kazue the next morning to spend a few hours walking around to hidden crafting gems. Before we started, she insisted I go to the nearest convenience store to buy an umbrella for the falling snow. She politely would not listen to my insistence that umbrellas are for rain, not snow, and that I was perfectly fine with a bit of snow.

She ended up being right about the umbrella, because the snow turned into slush dropping down from the sky. I would have been absolutely soaked.

Kazue runs these walking craft tours throughout Kyoto. This isn't some tourism-kickback tour. Given how artistic and creatively curious she is, you get the feeling that these hole-in-the-wall places are ones she's found for herself over the years. That she's letting you in on a few almost secret locations.

Are you a potter looking for inspiration and supplies? She'll bring you to modern studios, ateliers still doing the traditional techniques, and a plethora of supply stores.

When I told Kazue that I wanted to sew my own clothes eventually, she took on the assignment with gusto. We went down back alleys, into shops across the metro area. Basically everywhere.

As we walked, we chatted about crafts and creativity. About how transferable creative mindsets can be. That night, I kept thinking about our discussion: how the essence of a creative practice, as clichéd as it may sound, is joy and a beginner's mindset. You need joy to keep going. And you need a beginner's mindset to keep trying, flailing, and occasionally not flailing.

Everyone I'd met through Kazue's classes, both online and in person, were beginners. Most were foreigners. No one was an expert, and it would be a long time before any of us were. But plenty of the women made beautiful pieces of sashiko. Many had backgrounds in other crafts or types of stitching. You could see the skills transfer. Several remarked on how surprised they were that once shown a new way of doing something, they started seeing it everywhere.

That perspective showed up on Kazue's walking tour. She literally showed me a new way of seeing the city. One of the first places we went was down a narrow alley off a street I'd walked past a few times. I hadn't even registered it as an alley until Kazue started walking down it.

At the end of it was a door that opened onto the most picturesque courtyard. Imagine the kind of place where Bashō would've been writing his poems, and you've got a decent image of where we were. A perfectly manicured garden. Thick snow falling. A little back house with a big square window and a stone path through the garden to the front door. Inside was a man whose family has been making sewing needles for fourteen generations.

He had a display case with so many types of needles. I had kinda figured all needles were basically the same: some longer, some shorter, some pointier. As this man nicely explained, there is incredible nuance among needles. Some are made to bend a bit, letting you make curves more easily. Some are ridged. Some have big eyes for thicker thread, others smaller eyes for thinner thread. Some are for embroidery, others dressmaking, still others for sashiko.

By the end of his explanations of the needles, I was deeply impressed with them and quite overwhelmed with choice. I ended up with a small handful of needles, wrapped individually in little pieces of paper wrapping on which I wrote notes so I'd remember which needle was for which task.

We continued on. This time for scissors. I was slightly confused when we walked into a knife shop but trusted Kazue. It turns out, one of the best places to buy crafting scissors is in a knife shop.

Kazue was going to set me up right. The supplies, as she knew so well, really make a difference in any crafting project. And Japan makes the best craft supplies.

We walked some more and ended up down a random street not far from a main commercial drag I'd been before—another turn I had passed and not seen. So much of what delighted me about Kyoto this time around was just that: seeing new things in plain sight.

We got two pairs of scissors. The first were big cloth-cutting scissors that sliced through fabric with a smoothness I didn't realize scissors were capable of. Best of all, they fit my small(ish) hands perfectly.

The second scissors we found were thread snips. Again, I had assumed scissors are scissors. Why would I need one just for cutting thread? As Kazue explained, it's really nice to have a pair of small scissors that snip just right and make a good, clean cut.

The day kept going on like this with unexpected and wonderful shop after shop. We walked into what looked like a family's home but was actually an old sashiko thread shop with so many colors of thread, some shiny, some matte—all for sashiko stitching. We went into a shop literally stuffed to the ceiling with cut-up pieces of old kimonos and bedspreads, all ready to be sold and repurposed.

Kazue showed me the more modern side of Kyoto crafting, too. There was the wholesale store, the dyeing materials store, the multibuilding high-end fabric store.

We had lunch together, both of us eating a big bowl of soup to warm up from the snow. I had more sewing craft supplies than I knew what to do with and a deep excitement to make things with them. With each hidden alleyway, Kyoto started to intrigue me more and more. I understood what I had missed last time. I had missed the vibrancy, the depth of crafts, and the dedication to doing something really well—for generations.

I took the Shinkansen back down to Fukuoka. The zipper of my backpack almost didn't close because of all the new crafting supplies I'd shoved into it.

I tend to get a tad overenthusiastic about plans; I'm an optimist to a fault. I'm pretty sure I can do all the things, all at once, and have all the time in the world to do them. When Kazue proposed a new sashiko project to our online Zoom class, I was super excited to use all my new goodies.

She'd already shown it to me in Kyoto: a vintage placemat decorated with sashiko stitching she'd found at the flea market. The fabric was indigo-dyed cotton. The thread was thick, white sashiko thread. The pattern, Kakinohana, was the persimmon flower pattern I recognized, one of the simpler sashiko patterns to do.

My confidence was high—a bit too high, one might say. Because while the pattern was simple, the way I decided to go about it wasn't. I was getting a little bored with stitching for stitching's sake.

The unknown woman whose placemat we were copying wouldn't have used a kit, or even gridded fabric. Nor would she have drawn a grid herself. I thought, *Hey, I've gotten pretty good at sashiko stitching, let me get a bit creative with this one.* I still wanted to use a grid, but I figured I could experiment in other ways. I grabbed some fancy, colorful, design-y fabric I'd bought in Kyoto that was certainly not meant for sashiko stitching. It was thick, tightly woven, and had a nice circular pattern.

Pretty but in hindsight terrible for sashiko. Ideally, you work on thin fabric with a loose weave. It lets you easily make all those stitches. With my fancy fabric, each stitch was a struggle. I had to jam the needle through the fabric and then yank it out the other side. For each stupid stitch.

Worse yet, because of the pattern, I had trouble seeing my stitching grid. Each stitch was a pain—and I couldn't even see where they were supposed to go.

Not meditative. Not enjoyable. My mat was getting uglier with each row of stitches. The one Kazue had us copying was a lovely, simple piece, where the contrast between the white thread and blue background let the sashiko pattern shine. Mine was just muddling up the fabric and hiding the stitching.

I could have just started again, with the right supplies. I meant to do that. I told myself I'd totally restart the project and that it would be fun again.

But I started wondering: If the woman who had made the original placemat had had the option to be doing something else, would she have? Why was I doing this? Why was I spending two months re-creating a placemat I wasn't going to use?

I didn't want a placemat. The stitches were tiny and frustrating. While I intended to redo it properly, I just somehow couldn't be bothered.

Who knows about the woman who made the original placemat. Maybe she had no other choice or maybe she loved stitching it. Yes, fabric does hold memories. But once that person is gone, it's a lot harder to actually unlock those memories.

All my classmates clearly had the option to do something else. They were paying for classes, after all. Kazue was certainly a talented artist who could pursue a number of creative practices. There were obviously people who wanted to do sashiko purely out of artistic desire. But maybe that wasn't me?

My interest in sashiko, after all, hadn't been so much in sashiko itself, but rather in getting the hand-feel of sewing a straight line. Sashiko had taught me that. It didn't scratch the same itch that rows and rows of the knit stitch does for me.

When it came down to it, the end result felt too utilitarian for me. I mean, it's nice to have a few kitchen towels, but now I had four. How many does one really need? Especially if you're eating out all the time because you're living in foodie Fukuoka and have no time to cook because you've enrolled in an overly intense language school. Really, I only used the sashiko towels to wipe up the occasional coffee spill in the mornings before class.

I had gotten what I came for. I could do a tidy running stitch. Sashiko taught me how thread interacts with cloth, how color choices matter, how fabric and thread texture influence a project.

But I hadn't found a new creative practice I wanted to keep pursuing. If I ever did return to larger sewing projects, like making clothing, I'd be using those sashiko skills. For now, I wanted nothing to do with sewing. Or, honestly, being indoors at all.

The excitement of living in Fukuoka was starting to wear off. Sam and I had spent much of our time inside—in classrooms or in our apartment, studying. There just wasn't time for much else. The running loops around Ohori Park started to feel a bit mundane. It was still one of the coolest city parks I've ever been to, but it was still just a park. The mountains were visible from the city but took all day to reach. Same with the ocean: You could see it, but the places you'd actually want to swim weren't easy to get to.

Everything felt a bit more difficult than I'd imagined. I was starting to understand what I'd heard from other foreigners: Japan is a great place to visit, but it can be a hard place to live long-term.

I needed to get outside. I needed to move my body. I needed a wider definition of creativity. I needed to check out some other places in Japan.

We quit the language school. Sam went back to California for a bit. I went with him for a month and then reentered Japan on a tourist visa. I had an idea that would stretch my previous definition of craft.

Chapter 3

Cræft

I'm not someone who can work at a desk job. I've got to move. I get melodramatic and cranky at even the thought of being asked to show up to the same desk most days of the week. Even in college and graduate school, I had to switch up where I studied. I'd find different nooks around campus to hide away with my laptop and books. The small adventure of exploring new hidden areas helped alleviate some of the drudgery.

I was starting to feel the same way about sewing and knitting. Too much sitting. Not much action. Creative practices were supposed to expand my life, not make it smaller.

Over the past couple of years, I kept hearing about this other Japanese matrilineal culture, the ama. The ama don't paint. They don't write. They don't knit. But they've crafted a tradition that's deeply creative in its approach to income, food, gender roles, and daily life.

The ama are Japanese women who free dive, sea foraging for turban snails, lobsters, abalone, and other underwater delicacies. What they don't keep for themselves they sell to the fishermen's market. Their knowledge has been passed down through generations, grandmother to mother to daughter. They've been diving for somewhere between 3,000 and 5,000 years.

Even the *Manyoshu*, the oldest poetry anthology written in Japanese, has poems about the ama. Thought to be compiled by Ōtomo no Yakamochi, who was born in AD 718, the anthology contains thousands of poems, some significantly older than Yakamochi himself. The topics covered are the usual human scope of feelings expressed by poetry since time immortal: love, loss, celebration, death, and beauty. The ama show up in all these themes, including in one particularly melodramatic poem where diving for abalone—with their distinctive paired shells— becomes a metaphor for unrequited love.

There are also countless historical illustrations of ama in daily life. An illustrated encyclopedia from 1666 includes images of them. Woodblock prints, especially those by the artists Utamaro and Toyokuni, dating back to 1799 show ama and the ocean in the characteristic ukiyo-e style of bold colors and everyday life.

These aren't meek, vapid mermaids. These historical drawings depict powerful, life-loving, and often nude women working the ocean. The ama are clearly badass. But why include them in a book about creativity? Because I believe the ama engage in a deep creative practice, one as meaningful as the Danish knitwear designers and sashiko sewists. It's a creative tradition that is solely the domain of women. This matrilineal, sea-foraging expertise, passed down and practiced for millennia, embodies the very essence of creativity.

A creative practice, as I see it, doesn't have to result in making something physical, as much as I do like crafting useful things. It does require a generative lens, in the same way gardening, parenting, and farming can all be considered creative practices. The ama are generative not because they produce art or objects, but because they have a way of being rooted in production, tradition, and intentionality.

Before I had even met any ama, I already knew that their creative practice could be found in their approach.

I knew, too, that I was stuck in a recent—and too narrow—understanding of craft. I started getting existential about it. What is creativity? What is a practice? What is an act? Could I do a creative practice that resulted in nothing? The fun of knitting, after all, wasn't exactly getting a red sock, which I still hadn't finished. The end result was a welcome by-product of the act of knitting itself.

The archaeology book *Cræft: An Inquiry into the Origins and True Meaning of Traditional Crafts* caught me. Written in 2018 by the British archaeologist Alex Langlands, it got at what had been stumping me about my too-narrow definition of craft.

Langlands is clearly an archaeology nerd in the most delightful way—from 2009 to 2012 he cohosted several BBC historical working farm shows. He and his cohosts re-created life on working farms from different time periods. They didn't just play dress-up. They made the hay, plowed the fields, and grew the crops—using only the tools the Victorians, Edwardians, or World War II farmers would have had. This gave him a much deeper understanding of the past.

It also got him thinking about the relationship between doing things with your body and the larger world. Using historical tools gave him a new way of seeing the past and led him to him reconsider an Old English word similar to our term *craft* but ultimately is radically different: *cræft*.

Cræft is this mysterious term that pops up throughout Old English writings. We have a hard time directly translating it to modern English. It doesn't just refer to the act of weaving, blacksmithing, or hedge trimming. It also encompasses virtue, power, skill, wisdom, and context.

Cræft lives in the body as much as the mind. You can't learn it from books alone. It's embodied knowledge gained through failure, repetition, being in a specific environment, and a lineage of mentorship. Cræft is about doing something well with attention to tools and place.

Richard Sennett, the sociologist I mentioned in the first chapter, echoes this. In his book *The Craftsman,* he argues that craftsmanship is less about what you make than how you approach the process. Done well, woodworking, parenting, and software coding all require embodied knowledge gained through repetition, care, and curiosity. In Sennett's view, that's one of the best ways to engage with the world.

Free diving itself isn't necessarily a creative practice. But neither necessarily is the running stitch or a row of knitting. It's what you do with the skill that makes it creative. Free diving for food, as a lifestyle and lineage, is creative in the same way farming or cooking is creative.

The ama don't make sweaters; they're making food. Seaweed goes into soup. Abalone gets sold for cash, just like you might sell a hand-stitched quilt. A few turban snails might become a post-dive snack in a beach hut. Eating your own sea-foraged food is to a 7-Eleven snack what a handmade dress is to one bought at Target. Both technically serve the same function, but the process is radically different. It is the cræft that makes the difference.

My fascination with the ama may also, of course, be rooted in something more basic. I am a diver myself. And I'd recently learned to free dive.

The ama, like a lot of different cultures over the millennia, have figured out our biological secret—we are evolutionarily adapted to spend a lot of time in and under water. Did you know you can hold your breath longer underwater than you can on land? Even just splashing some water on your face can trigger this reflex.

Free diving takes advantage of this. You take a deep breath, dive down, hang out, and come up eventually—usually seconds or even minutes later.

On land, this very moment and without any training, you can probably hold your breath for about three minutes. Really truly. It's going to feel like you can't. You're going to panic, feeling like you can't reach the three-minute mark without dying. That's just your brain (nicely, understandably) freaking out, declaring that without a steady supply of oxygen you'll die. That's true, of course. The timeline is just much longer than your brain thinks it is.

There are historical records of people free diving for ten, twelve, fifteen minutes per breath. It's unclear if we've simply lost the techniques to stay down that long or if those times were slightly fudged over the years. But free divers are getting closer and closer to those large breath holds.

I'd been curious about free diving for years, and I finally learned in Indonesia, right before we moved to Fukuoka. Free diving is basically just extreme snorkeling. I wanted to be able to float comfortably on the ocean surface, then with a gentle body movement, glide down dozens of feet, hang out there, swim around, look at creatures, all while feeling calm and safe.

You can free dive kinda anywhere, but if I'm picking somewhere to jump into the ocean, it's going to be Indonesia. Over the last decade, I've spent my time in Indonesia hiking in jungles, diving in remote archipelagos, doing research in tiny villages.

I love the ocean. In or even near it my brain feels calm and expansive. Sam and I have long been scuba divers, often diving the ocean in Indonesia. There, it's deep, it's clear, and it's often rushing with currents and teeming with the craziest-looking creatures from tiny leafy, seaweed-looking sea dragons to gaint whale sharks.

I went into our free-dive lessons being like, *Yeah, no worries, I'm a pretty experienced scuba diver. I am comfortable at all sorts of depths. I signed us up for the best, safest free-diving school out there. I have this.*

I did not. I freaked out.

Free diving, it turns out, is a wildly different experience than scuba. Not breathing changes things. Free diving completely exposes you to the ocean. You feel the pressure and power of it. You feel your body being squeezed by the ocean's pressure. Gravity tangibly pulls your body down to the depths of the ocean, whether you're slowly falling with gravity or swimming to the surface against it.

I spent many of those first dives panicked, pretty sure I was setting myself up to be a great candidate for the Darwin

Awards, that awful Internet 1.0 list of people who died in dumb ways. Slowly I started to relax, to actually look around at where I was. I could still feel the pressure of the ocean on my throat as I sank myself down into the depths, but as my heartbeat slowed, the stranglehold lessened. I started to have fun.

By the end of our two months there, Sam and I could dive down to a hundred feet, hang out, and then come back up—rinse and repeat. We could hold our breath for minutes. We weren't just going down and coming back up, relieved to still be alive. We were playing with it. Angling our heads, tucking our chins to be even more streamlined vertically. Seeing how long we could dangle at the end of the rope. Looking out at the big blue ocean.

A few months after we left Indonesia, we went to a remote island in French Polynesia while we were still traveling. There we free dived with humpbacks. Swimming with the whales was this combination of awe, movement, and being in a totally different environment—of being in the whales' space, not ours.

The whales are completely in control of their interactions with you. If they wanna come close, they'll bring their big eyes and bodies to you. If not, it's a quick body movement and the whale disappears into the blue.

Sometimes, if you're lucky, a whale might decide to hang out with you for a while. Compared to a whale, you're a tiny little thing. You maintain a respectful distance, but the whale might not—it might come zooming over to you, looking through its big eyes at you. Its eyes look extremely human, just incredibly large.

This is why I learned to free dive—to engage with the ocean, to play with it, to experience another realm of our world. The skills I gained from learning the sport of free diving let me do creative things with it. Free diving was utterly about process and intentionality while moving my body. The thing was, I still wanted utility. Going up and down a rope in the middle of the ocean is incredibly meditative. I wanted to do something with that skill.

As I swam with the whales, I started to wonder a lot about the ama. These were women, after all, who paired something I absolutely love—being in the water with sea life—with a creative act, foraging. That combination seemed extremely exciting.

As our time in Fukuoka came to an end, I set about trying to learn as much as possible about the ama, with the hope that maybe one day I might be able to free dive with them.

I made my way to an ama hotspot: Toba City in Shima Peninsula of Mie Prefecture. From Tokyo I took multiple trains to Ujiyamada Station in Mie. There I stuffed my mask and fins in the trunk of an adorable little kei car and started driving through Ise-Shima National Park, past forested mountains and a rocky coastline. Online I had booked a somewhat random hotel. It turned out to have an *onsen* in the basement, delicious multicourse locally caught seafood dishes, and views of the sea so amazing that I felt immersed in the ocean. The next morning, I got back in the Kie and kept driving.

I continued driving through the national park, took a left turn down a small road, and followed it to a seeming dead end. There, in literally the middle of nowhere Japan, is the Toba Sea Folk Museum, a huge multibuilding museum complex (over 40,000 square feet) dedicated to the ama and other traditions of engaging with the ocean in Japan.

As soon as you walk inside the main building, you see multiple life-size ama suspended from the ceiling, giving museum visitors the feeling of being on the ocean floor looking up at an ama diving down. Immediately, you understand just how deep ama go on each of their dives—it's an eye-catching, dramatic way to start your museum trip.

That drama is on purpose. Every bit of the museum is designed to give you a feeling of being in and around the sea. The layout is explicitly route-less, like being in the ocean. You meander based on what catches your eye, get caught in a back corner by some interesting infographic and then swept across the room by a replica ama hut beckoning you. Angles of the walls and ceiling are curved, not straight, and meant to mimic ocean waves. The award-winning architect, Hiroshi Naito, purposely added varied ceiling heights with exposed wooden trusses and skylights for extra sealike unpredictability.

One building holds over eighty archival boats. You take your shoes off and quietly walk around the building, which is lit only by skylight to help preserve the boats. It feels like visiting a boat graveyard.

This was clearly not the dusty little one-room tired display I was expecting. It was vibrant, full of schoolkids running around. Every time we ran into each other, the little middle-schoolers wanted to practice their English, proud to tell me that they knew ama—their aunts, grandmothers, and moms. That they were thinking about becoming an ama when they grew up. That they were from Japan and that's where the ama are from.

I learned about the ama's different chisel options for removing abalone from rocks and how these have evolved over time. I read detailed infographics about the measuring gauge that ama always carry to make sure the abalone they're harvesting is big enough (over 10.6 centimeters, about four years old) to be an environmentally sustainable catch. I saw the different types of goggles ama have used over the years and learned that they are a relatively recent addition to the ama toolkit—and that goggles were a quite controversial addition when first introduced, with many ama questioning if goggles gave them an unfair advantage against the ocean.

I also learned that the ama have two talismans that they draw, embroider, and hammer onto their clothes and tools— the Dōman and Seiman. Both are somewhat common good-luck symbols within Japanese culture.

The first symbol, the *Dōman*, is made up of four vertical lines and five horizontal ones that look like a mega-hashtag. This symbol is a physical version of the Buddhist Kuji-in ("Nine-Hand Seals")—nine different hand gestures and mantras often done to gather spiritual forces against evil and usually performed for luck. Makes sense that the ama would want this symbol on everything possible.

The second, the *Seiman*, is a single-line star that was used as the personal seal of Abe no Seimei, who, born in AD 921, worked as an Onmyōji—a Japanese court official who served the emperor by specializing in magic and divination. Abe no Seimei is perhaps the most famous Onmyōji in Japan—he's still a big deal today. He appears as a beloved character in novels, anime, and video games. There's even an asteroid named after him.

It's thought that because the Seiman star begins where it ends, there's no place for evil spirits to enter. Which is good because the ama have a lot to contend with underwater, including demons: the *Sanshoubirashi* ("organism that stings"), *Boushin* ("ghost boat"), *Hikimouren* ("sea ghost"), and *Shirikoboshi* ("monster that takes liver out from anus"). The *Tomokazuki* is an underwater demon that looks like an ama but won't have any Seiman or Dōman on her stuff. She'll appear friendly and gesture as if she just wants to show you something a bit farther down in the ocean. Or, even more tempting, she'll try to hand you an abalone. Accept that prize catch or follow her deep into the ocean and she'll eventually drown you.

One of the things Alex Langlands emphasized in his book about cræft is that tools are never stand-alone objects. Understanding that an ama feels like she might face a demon underwater is as important as knowing what type of bucket, chisel, or wetsuit she uses.

The more I learned about the ama and their craft, the more I became intrigued. I wanted to know more about these women who can dive down deep and sea forage.

I needed to go meet some real-life ama.

Chapter 4

Duck Dives

Some of the older ama want nothing to do with tourists, like me, who have lots of questions. After a hike along a semi-technical trail to a beach spot with a cluster of ama huts, I encountered one eighty-year-old woman who rolled up on her motorcycle wearing blue-gray leopard print rain boots. She curtly answered a few questions from me and my translator, Akiko Tanaka, but then gestured at the firewood on the back of her motorcycle, indicating that she had other things to do. We said goodbye and she carried that firewood to her metal-roofed beach hut where, like all ama do, she'll eat, rest, and store her gear pre- and post-dives.

But then again, as I'd come to learn, the ama aren't what you'd expect. Even though I knew they were badass, I didn't realize just how much.

Like most craftspeople, the ama aren't always the most outgoing. They're not just going to hand you their techniques. This attitude is somewhat out of secrecy, but also from a deep bodily knowledge that really can only be experienced to be understood.

At the museum I had seen exhibits of the huts where the ama rest, prep their gear, and cook the shellfish they're not selling. The cool thing is that the ama still use them. Some of these huts are even open to tourists. That's how most outsiders meet the ama. They go to curated lunches hosted by older ama interested in sharing their stories and shaping how the wider world sees them.

Many ama I talked to told me that they feel misunderstood by foreigners. Outsiders come expecting mermaids: happy-go-lucky, sexualized, ageless women who are one with the sea and also somehow demure. That stereotype misses everything. How strong the ama are. How much they risk their lives every day. Why they care so much about being in the sea. Why they care so much about being financially independent.

Working at a tourism hut lets the older ama directly control the narrative and it subsidizes their income. By working as an ama you can make decent money if you find the right things. Abalone is the biggest cash cow, coming in at 10,000 to 30,000 yen apiece (70 to 200 USD). But that's only for the big, undamaged ones. Most of the time, these days, being an ama doesn't pay well.

At these tourism huts, tourists pay to eat lunch cooked by the ama themselves. At one, Nakaseko Mie (sixty years old) and Misako Uemura (seventy-seven) welcomed me into a smoky, calm space. In the center of the hut, they roasted oysters, sea cucumber, turban snails, abalone, spiny lobster, and sea urchin over a charcoal fire pit.

Nakaseko wore squishy black sandals with toe socks—each toe a bright green, the rest of the sock gray. Misako wore bright orange Crocs. Like the leopard print boot-wearing ama I had previously met, both had arrived at the hut by motorcycle and had been diving for decades. As Nakaseko put it: "I've been diving since I was inside my mother."

Two other tourists joined me for lunch: a couple from Tokyo with their little yappy white dog. The dog barked at the shellfish and Nakaseko barked back, laughing.

As Misako prepared the still-alive spiny lobster for one of the women of the couple, she asked if the tourist wanted to skewer it herself. The woman nervously took the skewer and lobster. She hesitated and started apologizing profusely to the lobster, saying *I'm so sorry to do this to you*, and couldn't bring herself to stab it. Misako laughed, took the lobster back, and in one swift motion skewered it and set it roasting over the charcoal. *It's fiiiiiiiiiiine*, she said. *The lobster is tasty. Just eat it.*

I was glad it wasn't me being asked to stab a lobster. I felt brave enough pretending I was enthusiastic about slurping the turban snails out of their shells, green goo and all.

At another tourist hut (I went to a couple—it turns out

turban snails taste pretty good), Kimiyo Hayashi (sixty-nine years old) made my lunch. She had a deeply lined face with bright, twinkling eyes.

Her husband built her an ama hut near the ocean in the 1970s, and she's been using it ever since. But, as Kimiyo explained, she had taken a detour first: As a high-schooler, she traveled to San Diego to be part of a SeaWorld exhibit called Japan Village, where ama performed diving demonstrations. She told me she loved it. Kimiyo had grown up diving in a family of ama. In California, she got to be in the water and be a young adult far away from the watchful eyes of her parents. Eventually, though, she returned to Mie and the more traditional ama lifestyle.

Kimiyo's abalone, clams, and everything else were expertly prepared with metal tongs over a charcoal fire pit in the middle of the hut. We ate lunch together there, but afterward she brought me back to her real working hut—the one her husband had built her.

The tourism hut was curated: kitschy details, smiling photographs of ama at the beach. Kimiyo's working hut was controlled chaos: drying wetsuits, piled gear, bundles of firewood. There was space to prep for dives and to relax afterward. Her old-school hut felt like the huts I had seen in the museum, just updated to have a sturdier roof and walls.

But, standing there, I wondered: Where did the ama my age gather?

When I went into Osatsu Cafe Sen in Toba City, I didn't realize it was an ama-dominated space. I was hungry for lunch and the food looked good. It turned out to be a modern, hip cafe owned and staffed by ama, with other ama casually hanging out at nearby tables. I had stumbled into a contemporary version of the old-school ama hut.

The food was almost the same as what I'd been served in the ama tourism huts. Delicious. While the ama at the tourism huts tended to be older, the women at Osatsu Cafe Sen were in their late thirties and forties: millennials and Gen X. These younger ama were also explicitly interested in controlling the narrative of what it means to be ama—and had likely become ama because of the work done by the older generation.

As I'd learn, most of this younger generation didn't grow up in ama families or even in the region. Many had moved here to Mie Prefecture. They all did it for love—be it the love of a man or the love of the sea (or both). They like the sisterhood aspect of it. The being in the ocean. The addiction of the hunt. The creating their own schedules. A life where you don't have to fit yourself into a man's world and choose between being a woman and having a career. Where it's a woman-dominated field. Where women are financially independent. Where women risk their lives in the sea every time they go in. Where women are steering the narrative of their lives.

But, as these women are getting into this new career, the seas are also changing. Abalone, the main prey of the ama, are diminishing in numbers.

Figuring out how to financially stay afloat is a big deal for every single ama. The money just isn't what it used to be. So they're figuring out what it means to be an ama, to continue the tradition while also adjusting to modernity. Luckily, they're in a tradition that has been walking that line for a long time.

Beyond food for purchase at Osatsu Cafe Sen, there's a whole section of ama-made goods. Everything from ama-themed earrings to soaps to ama dolls to seaweed. It helps the younger generation diversify their income streams.

For the ama, you'd think this was their creative outlet. It kinda is. But it clearly is more merch than *cræft*. These goods are a means to an end and feel different than sashiko cloths or the sweaters I'd seen women knitting in Denmark.

The ama were clearly proud of their merchandise. But when we chatted, they were more excited to show me photos of their dives and catches than the merch for sale. The gift shop stuff was clearly for extra cash so that they could keep diving.

I bought two tenugui cloths, lightweight cotton towels that are useful for everything from kitchen spills to a makeshift headband on a humid day. They featured illustrations of ama divers, abalone, and the Dōman and Seiman symbols.

I spoke with Rikako Sato, the ama designer of the cloths. Like many younger ama, she didn't grow up by the sea. She moved here for love. Her husband, a fisherman and marine biologist from Nagoya, wanted to live near the ocean. They agreed on a move to a small town by the sea, near-ish to where Osatsu Cafe Sen is located.

Rikako didn't want to have an office job where she had to choose between being a mother and having a career. When her new neighbor suggested Rikako become an ama, the work-life balance intrigued her. She became an ama for what it offered her as a career and life option—a woman-dominated field focused on independence and strong, gusty women who are often mothers.

It's also a field that doesn't pay a lot. Rikako has spent a lot of time thinking about an all-encompassing view of what it means to be an ama. One that is, yes, about catching specific creatures, but also broader than that. That it is about a specific lifestyle where you're in and near the ocean. Where you make your money from being in the ocean. But maybe that just also means selling things like ama-themed tenugui cloths or being an Instagram influencer or running a guest house as a way to make enough money to continue being an ama.

Rikako sees being an ama as bigger than just hunting abalone in a way that seems to align with the encompassing definition of cræft. For Rikako, the ama tradition is a love of being in and near the ocean. A sisterhood. A lifestyle.

Even if you can get an ama to pause and chat, it turns out you can't just go diving with them. There are permits, regulations, and all sorts of rules of who can forage when and where.

I had spent months emailing back and forth with the Ise-Shima Tourism Board to arrange a dive with an ama. On the long-awaited day, I drove my tiny rental car to a boat harbor at the literal end of the road in Kashikojima.

There, I met Naoko Sugiyama, an ama not much older than myself, to go sea foraging. Like Rikako and most of the younger ama I met on this trip, Naoko did not grow up in the area and didn't come from a long line of ama. She was born in Hokkaido, where she loved pool swimming as a kid on that cold northern island. As soon as she could, she moved to the opposite end of Japan: Okinawa. There she worked in the dive industry and relished the tropical waters. A handful of years ago, she moved to Mie with her husband and two kids for the explicit purpose of becoming an ama.

She was every bit the badass I had imaged the ama to be. Honestly, they all were. Never have I had such high expectations for a group and had them not just met but exceeded.

Once again, I found myself ready to duck dive down into unknown waters. When you're free diving in crystal-clear Indonesia water along a rope, you tuck your chin. You stare at the ocean, at the rope, at nothing. It almost doesn't matter whether you open your eyes.

Not so when sea foraging with the ama. You're actively looking. You're hunting. It's not just you and a seemingly empty ocean. There are plants, coral, rocks, seaweed, fish, shelled critters, animals. Some you want to catch. Others you need to avoid.

Together with a translator and a member of the Ise-Shima Tourism Board, Naoko and I got into a small motorboat and headed out. As we sat in the boat, the four of us chatted while Naoko and I put on our dive gear. We both wore nice wetsuits. I borrowed mine from the Ise-Shima Tourism Board. (The one I'd brought was deemed not warm enough.) Naoko, with her scuba-diving background, had her own modern, well-worn wetsuit, but her tools looked like they belonged in the Toba Sea Folk Museum.

When we arrived at our foraging spot, Naoko hopped off the side of the boat with a buoy, rope, and what looked like a rusty crowbar. I followed, hesitating slightly.

I've done the motion so many times: roll off the side of the boat, splash into the water, and descend into another world. I love that feeling. But this was different. I was kinda nervous.

To make it a fair fight against the ocean, the ama use the old-school gear I'd learned so much about at the museum. It's the antithesis of industrial trawling where giant boats scoop up everything, killing more than will be eaten.

Their tools for things like prying and scraping the abalone off rocks are often rusty and old. Even their wetsuits are worn and patched. The whole point of being an ama is maintaining a deep, sustained relationship with the ocean—to be of and in it. A hole in your wetsuit? If it's not bothering you, who cares? The tools just need to work. No need for flashy new gear or ounce-counting like today's outdoor gear culture (of which I'm as guilty as the next person).

Safety is . . . loose. Every ama's relationship with ropes terrified me. Most tie a rope to a buoy floating on the surface, either holding the rope, like Naoko does, or (even more terrifying) tying it around their waist. The buoy alerts nearby boats about the diver and has a net for the ama to stash her catch as she continues diving.

Loose ropes in and near water get tangled. Knotted. Caught. If your rope snags and you can't get free of a tangle, you drown. Every ama I met had either had a close call or knew someone who had drowned. Every single one.

Kimiyo, the ama who'd worked at SeaWorld, laughed as she told me she was nearly run over twice by the same guy in a boat. Both times, she saw the boat just in time, let go of her buoy's rope, and dove deep down underwater. Her buoy was destroyed, but she was fine. After the second time, he brought her a liter of sake as an apology. As she told me the story, she thought it was funny. I doubt she did in the moment.

Add to all this that ama often dive solo, with others nearby-ish. (Naoko was being generous in letting me tag along.) It's not the free-diving buddy system I had gotten used to in Indonesia, where one person dives and the other watches. Ama diving is almost territorial: *Stay out of my area, I'm hunting here. We can hang as friends later but not right now.* If you got stuck underwater, no one might see you.

Same if you black out. Technically, ama do safety breaths between dives. These are purposeful big gulps of air and relaxed exhales to make sure you re-oxygenate yourself. Safety breaths can be literally lifesaving and take all of twenty seconds.

But safety breaths are easy to skip. Most free-diving deaths don't occur during deep record attempts. They happen to spearfishers and foragers in shallow water. They're alone or with no one super nearby, and they're focused on the hunt and not realizing that they're running out of air. These shallow-water blackouts usually happen just below the surface. It's a quiet, mundane death. They die by slipping into unconsciousness, having not realized how fatigued they were.

It happens frighteningly easily. When you're focused too much on the hunt, it's easy to pop up and down as much and as fast as you can.

After all, there's a clock ticking. The ama unions (yes, there are unions) heavily regulate when, where, and who can go ama diving. Out of the six-month diving season, Naoko said she probably only gets in the water about seventy days. There are scheduled rest days (Tuesdays and Saturdays), festivals, ceremonies, and unexpected bad weather. The easiest time to find an ama on land and available to chat? Rainy, windy days.

I thought about all this as I floated in the water. Naoko dove a few times while I watched. After three quick pop-downs, she paused and looked over at me. *Why are you not diving?* she asked.

I ducked dived down with her and she pointed out where among the tendrils of seaweed she was looking. I stared hard and saw nothing we'd want to forage. She swam closer to the spot and picked up a turban snail, hiding in plain sight. If it hadn't been in her hand, I still wouldn't have seen the snail. I floated there and wondered what else I wasn't seeing. My nerves increased.

The water was surprisingly cold, and I was diving headfirst into murky water full of seaweed and plants, trying to spot something hidden on the seafloor or clinging to a rock. It's a little scary—because, well, what if there's something you don't want to find hiding in the seaweed? And what if you get tangled up in the buoy rope or seaweed? I understood why the ama took their underwater demon superstitions so seriously.

After a few dives, I relaxed and started having fun. The underwater world turned into a spectacle of colors. Seaweed swayed. Coral popped with brightness. Fish darted about.

In sea foraging you're trying to maintain that intentional, balanced state as much as possible. If you spot an abalone, you need to pry it off its rock without damaging the creature. Abalone aren't static. They move. They suction tightly to rocks. Miss your chance on the first try and the abalone will clamp down ever harder, making it nearly impossible to get off.

Naoko told me that when she sees a really good abalone but can't harvest it on the first try, she'll surface, take a moment to relax, and then go back down. It lets her refocus. And usually by then, the abalone has loosened its grip.

You have to sea forage with this type of open-eyed calm. That type of seeing lets you see the shine of a shell on a rock and the subtle shift in seaweed color. It also helps you stay underwater longer. Staying calm extends your dive. Panic cuts it short.

When my brain starts to race, I try to bring it into the present moment by noticing. It's a basic mindfulness trick that is tremendously helpful when I remember to do it. I double down on noticing.

When sport free diving, I often focus my thoughts on my bodily sensations to calm down. But with sea foraging, I found I had to turn that awareness outward. I started playing around with other senses—what I could see, instead of what I could feel. If I panic, I literally lose the ability to see. So I tried to see *more*.

When you're sea foraging, you're moving slowly. You can watch how the light hits the particles in the water. It shimmers and dances. Sunbeams stream down, catching bits of sand, algae, and all the tiny pieces of ocean matter floating alongside you.

When you take that wide, slow view, the ocean reveals itself as anything but empty. I can pause and see the ocean pulsing around me. Holding your breath—on purpose—lets you pause in the world.

Free diving, whether for sport or foraging, lets you experience the ocean as alive. It's not just a backdrop. It's an animate world, full of nuance and depth. Like us, it's one thing made up of a bazillion other things. Pausing underwater, you can see how the ocean is both a singular and a plural, at the same time. You literally see the oneness and multiplicity of the ocean.

Air is like this, too. We experience it as empty, but it's crowded with microscopic life: bacteria, fungi, viruses, spores, and pollen, all mostly invisible to us. The nothingness is an illusion.

There's a moment—on just a few dives, not all—when you're ascending and the world completely stills. You feel extreme bliss and oneness. Something clicks. It's a bit like what I imagine long-term meditators describe.

Even if you don't surface transcendent or with a trophy abalone catch, free diving is just plain fun. It's cool to exist underwater like a fish. To be able to pop down and hang out in the ocean's thickness. To be in it. Not just observing but part of it. To feel like a fish, among the fish.

As beautiful as this whole thing was, I was hopeless at actually catching anything. If dinner depended on my foraging, we'd be hungry. In the murky water, I couldn't find a thing. Naoko, on the other hand, pulled up turban snails the size of her fist.

On the boat ride back to the harbor, Naoko smiled and told me it took her three years to get good at finding things in the ocean as an ama. Because first, she said, she had to learn how to see the ocean.

I asked Naoko, who used to work in tropical Okinawa's dive industry, why she'd move up here to kinda chilly Mie to work a physically hard job that, yes, sometimes pays but increasingly doesn't. Ama die on the job every year. There's no retirement plan. No subsidized sick days. No phoning it in. If you don't catch things, you don't make money.

She paused, then told me: She loves the thrill of the hunt. Being an ama is really fun. Addictive. Anytime she thinks about quitting, it pulls her back. It allows her to play in the ocean and be creative with how she lives as a Japanese woman.

That's why women keep choosing this life, right? Because it's a fun existence full of deliberate purpose. It's hard work, of course. But it's not drudgery. It's not someone else telling you what to do or who you can be. It's choosing yourself—and adventure.

As an ama, these women get to be in the sea every day. They have this tight-knit community of other women, older and younger. They share a deep connection to a specific place. They eat amazing food they've harvested themselves. They set their own schedules. Taking care of a sick kid doesn't require permission from a boss. They decide their own lives in a country that still often tells women what roles they can play: be a "working woman" or be a mother.

I mean, who wouldn't want that? Agency, ocean adventures, deep intentionality, a community of strong women, and tasty seafood.

I wanted to create that, without moving to rural Japan or becoming an ama. I wanted aspects of it. I wanted the highlights, without committing years to a single craft in a single place. Which, yes, I understand, is a very American approach that somewhat misses the point of a long-running Japanese creative practice.

What was it that intrigued me about the ama's lifestyle, if it wasn't that I was ready to quit everything and move to Mie? What was it about their specific approach to creativity that jibed with me?

I thought back to the archaeologist Langland's approach to cræft and the sociologist Sennett's understanding of craftsmanship. As Sennett writes, "The carpenter, lab technician, and conductor are all craftsmen because they are dedicated to good work for its own sake. Theirs is practical activity, but their labor is not simply a means to another end. The carpenter might sell more furniture if he worked faster; the technician might make do by passing the problem back to her boss; the visiting conductor might be more likely to be rehired if he watched the clock. It's certainly possible to get by in life without dedication. The craftsman represents the special human condition of being engaged."

A dedication to process while still caring about the outcome. Doing "good work for its own sake," but not only for the sake of doing it. The ama weren't just catching sea creatures. They weren't just free diving to put dinner on the table. Plenty of people spearfish without the craftsmanship of the ama.

As I started up my kei car, ready to start my long journey home from Mie, I glanced over to the passenger seat. There, I had placed a cleaned-up abalone shell from dinner at the hotel where I had been staying. The kitchen staff had heard about my time with the ama and made sure to serve me turban snails and abalone. I rarely ate my dinners alone. So many of the female hotel staff would come by, curious, asking me questions about the ama: *Were they really as impressive as the stories say?*

The hotel played an eclectic instrumental soundtrack. One evening, as I chatted with a woman who, like many working in Japan's hospitality industry, had moved to Japan from China for better wages and the allure of a bigger life, the instrumental version of "Girls Just Wanna Have Fun" started playing. And really, that's it, isn't it?

You can theorize all you want, but at the end of the day, cræft is fun. It feels good to live a life filled with intention and adventure.

Chapter 5

Natality

After Fukuoka, Sam had returned to California. It's our vague home base when we're not quite sure where to go next. We've spent a lot of time in Los Angeles, where Sam grew up, but decided to try the Bay Area for its abundance of nature and friends. As I was hanging with the ama, Sam was looking at rental listings and starting to sort through our storage unit.

We weren't sure how long we'd stay—but knew we wanted to stay long enough for at least a rental lease, not just a month-to-month sublet. After I finished diving with the ama, I joined Sam in the Bay Area. That's when we decided to start trying to have a baby, and I got pregnant right away. We were so excited—and adamant that this tiny adventure buddy would only, could only, be an additive to our lives.

Adamant, because that isn't always how motherhood gets framed. After heartily congratulating me on being pregnant, one of my close friends sighed and said, *Are we really this age now? We're the parents?*

I suppose that could have hurt my feelings, but it didn't. I knew what she meant. Some of my close friends have kids, but many don't. There's this lingering cultural narrative that becoming a mother means the fun is over. Give up your play and become a grown-up. I remember when one of my oldest friends told me she was pregnant a few years ago. It was right in that transition moment between *Oh no, what are you going to do?* and *Congratulations, you probably really want this!* I almost said the same thing to her that my friend said to me: *So, you have to become a grown-up now?*

The thing is, I don't feel grown-up. I don't intend to feel grown-up. I've felt responsible most of my life, but that's never been the same thing.

To me, being "grown-up" connotes stagnation, and resignation—the finality within the phrase. That you're done growing, exploring, adventuring. That the curiousness is done.

That's the opposite of what I was after with this creativity exploration—and certainly the opposite of how I intended to be a pregnant person, much less a creative mother.

Here I was given a wonderful way to expand my thinking (even as my body started to expand). I could frame it as myself first—gotta put on your own gas mask—but it also nudged me beyond myself. Sometimes getting out of your own way helps.

Thinking about how I wanted to introduce this little human to the world helped me keep thinking about how I wanted to interact with the world as well.

Having this kid, I realized, might deepen my creativity and play—not limit it.

Almost all the women I'd interacted with on my creative adventures were mothers, grandmothers, or women who planned to become mothers. So many of the ama had chosen that life precisely because it let them be their adventurous selves and still raise children. To be independent and interdependent. For them, motherhood wasn't a boundary. It was a creative expansion. As with poetry, the constraints became generative.

When Sam and I would stay up late imagining life with a kid, we wondered what parts of ourselves we might pass along. Music and math were Sam's first thoughts. Mine were hiking and free diving.

We talked about how old a kid needs to be to travel deep into jungles (old enough to get the necessary vaccines), to trek high mountain trails (old enough to say "I feel weird" if altitude sickness hits). We even looked up when free-diving courses start (four years old).

But I surprised myself by also thinking about what I might knit for the baby. How snuggly a soft, hand-knit sleep suit might feel—both for the baby and for me, snuggling them. I imagined those tiny hands, still forming inside me, someday big enough to (clumsily, at first) hold knitting needles and knit their own clothes.

Ever since not knitting that red sock in the Amazon, I had been thinking about a life of creativity. Mostly my own. I'd been thinking about it as a solo act, even as I craved creative community.

But what if I could use this as a way to expand my creative community?

I thought about the ama, helping each other be financially independent, creative mothers. Then I thought back to those Danish women knitting outside cafes—chatting with friends with kids nearby.

I had questions for those hip knitting ladies, especially now that I was imagining my life as a parent. Knitting is almost as far from sea foraging as you can get in terms of adrenaline. But, from a distance, both communities seemed to share something: a deep, intentional approach to life.

Knitting would keep being part of my life. But I also wanted what came with it: the community and the other side effects that go beyond ending up with a sweater.

Ever since Fukuoka, I'd wanted to be knitting along with others, but I hadn't been able to find a community that fit. Still, I wanted to be knitting, so I looked at patterns online.

I bought a PDF pattern called Sailor Sweater, designed by Danish knitter Anne Ventzel, one of a cohort of Danish knitwear designers who sell their patterns online. For three months, I had been making slow, start-and-stop progress on it—usually alone at night, listening to an audiobook. I picked it for new skills I'd learn, like the boat neckline, and for the gentle, geometrically bumpy stripes lining the body and the sleeves. To me it was the kind of sweater you could throw over jeans, add earrings and hip sneakers, and be ready for a nice restaurant in California without looking like you tried too hard.

Seemingly every pattern I wanted to knit, including the Sailor Sweater, was created by a Danish designer. Denmark is the current epicenter of knitwear design and probably home to the most knitters per capita. Nearly all the major knitwear designers today live in this tiny country. They market their patterns on Instagram and sell them through personalized SquareSpace websites. Some of them earn most—or all—of their household income from these PDF patterns.

I'm talking about hundreds of thousands of Instagram followers popular. One designer, Mette Wendelboe Okkels, has over one million followers (the number is higher each time I check) and a staff of ten employees.

These designers, like Mette, aren't making patterns for top fashion houses, although some used to in past careers. They're designing sweaters for regular people who want to knit at home. It's mostly sweaters. A ton of beautiful sweaters, each pattern selling for around $7.

The sweaters are the clothing equivalent of Nordic interior design: simple yet elegant. A kind of wearable hygge.

The yarns they recommend are soft and strong, available in a rainbow of colors, but the favorites are muted and deep.

Their highly curated Instagrams show where you too could be knitting and wearing these stylish hygge sweaters: at the chilly Danish beachside with your kids playing nearby, at the museum wearing your art while looking at art, at home on the couch snuggling your fluffy dog, or at a sidewalk cafe, knitting with equally stylish friends.

No wonder their Instagram accounts are blowing up. These designers give you an Insta snapshot of an ideal existence and then sell you the way to make (and wear) that creative, beautiful lifestyle. All for $7 plus supplies.

I convinced the most creative person I know to go on a trip to Denmark with me: my little sister, Fiona. We had a sisters trip on the books, and I had been telling her for years that she'd love the design, food, and yarn shops of Copenhagen. I flew from the Bay Area and she from Brooklyn for a trip whose itinerary consisted of as many yarn shops and pastries as we could muster.

I figured if anyone could help me understand what a life of community, creativity, and general fun might look like, it would be Fiona.

My sister has always been creative. Even as a kid, she was constantly making things. These days, she runs operations for small, artist-driven, female-led creative companies (she's a math whiz) and does professional-level ceramics on the side—

as well as sewing, knitting, woodworking, and just about everything else.

When I was in third grade, we had a class assignment to bring in our favorite thing for show-and-tell. Kids brought in toys and books. I brought in three-year-old Fiona, with her bright blonde pigtails and bangs. She sat on a stool while I gave my presentation on how great she is and all the things I love about her.

I still feel the same way.

Back then, she probably wore her favorite outfit: a dress with a swishy skirt for twirling and brightly patterned leggings for climbing things. That's my sister—a wonderful combination of style, creativity, and adventure. At five foot two, she's still a tiny thing but can out-adventure most. She's mountaineered on glaciers in Patagonia and winters in Montana (for the skiing). Need something built, sewn, knitted, or otherwise made? Fiona either already knows how or can figure it out with some time.

She usually looks good while doing it, too. You might find her in the backcountry wilderness, covered with dirt and smiling. Or you might see her stylishly dressed, speaking French at a Parisian cafe. Her Brooklyn apartment feels like a boutique hotel: reclaimed tiles on the kitchen walls, curated art, a bundle of eucalyptus hanging from the shower head for a burst of fresh scent when the water runs hot.

Fiona is a great adventure partner. I couldn't wait to explore Copenhagen with her.

Fiona and I had compiled a list of Copenhagen yarn shops, bakeries, and restaurants from friends, the internet, and my previous trip to the city. Happily, it was far too long to complete in one week's visit.

We left our Airbnb and headed toward the first yarn shop on our list: Bruun Strik. It's just down the street from two iconic Danish bakeries—Meyers Bageri and Hart Bageri—along a wide boulevard with roomy sidewalks, protected bike lanes, and five-story stone buildings that practically scream idyllic European city.

Take the boulevard, Gammel Kongevej, in one direction and you'll end up near the Frederiksberg Gardens and Søndermarken Park: 158-ish acres of trees, playgrounds, blooming flowers, workout zones, a slowly flowing river, and grassy lawns for napping and picnicking. Head the other way and you'll pass boutique shops selling stylish used clothing and cafes with sidewalk seating, and eventually reach what the Danes call "the Lakes." These are four connected reservoirs filled with ducks, swans, and swan boats. A dirt path loops around them, often busy with walkers, runners, and strollers at all hours.

It was gently raining as we walked the twenty minutes to Bruun Strik. Fiona laughed and said, "Oh, so this is why the Danish knitwear designers make summer sweaters."

Bruun Strik is everything you'd imagine a Danish yarn shop to be: full of yarn, sure, but also light-filled and calm, staffed by young women eager to help you but also content to knit behind the counter as you touch seemingly every skein of yarn in the shop. Which is good, because that's exactly what Fiona did.

The store has an open floor plan. The walls are lined with cubbies overflowing with yarn in every color and texture. That's just the display yarn. Skeins and skeins of each variety are stocked in the back room, hidden behind a large curtain.

It's a lot to take in. I did a few laps with Fiona, then collapsed on their couch. The first-trimester symptoms were hitting me hard, hence the collapse onto the couch. There was no way I was going to be able to get off the couch and touch all the yarn options. Fiona took charge. She wasn't going to let me skip finding a knitting project just because I didn't feel like moving.

Above and beside the couch hung sample sweaters, examples of what you could knit with the yarn in the shop. I wanted to knit every single one. It was the curated Instagrams of Danish knitwear come to life. I recognized many of the sweater designs from my online searches, including some I had considered before ultimately choosing the Sailor Sweater.

Fiona pointed out an incredibly charming baby outfit—a sleep suit with a hood, mittens, booties, and five buttons—

designed by Mette. We decided that I absolutely needed to make it.

Fiona and one of the employees discussed the yarn options. (Helpfully, the employee had recently made the same sleep suit pattern for a friend's baby.) Merino? Mohair? Cashmere? Cotton? Alpaca? Fiona brought me each type to feel. The alpaca's softness won. It felt luxurious and sturdy enough for baby wear. I wanted to be wrapped in it. I figured my baby would, too.

Next, Fiona brought over the color options. Did I want something playful or more neutral?

As we lay the skeins of alpaca yarn out on the coffee table, a very pregnant mom and her six-year-old son joined us on the couch. They'd just bought yarn to make him a sweater to celebrate that he was about to become a big brother. His mom had decided on the type; he'd pick the colors. He looked so proud—of his new role and of the yarn he'd picked, a rich, light pink merino and a speckled, almost tie-dye alpaca.

Danes don't gender colors as intensely as Americans do. Even we Americans haven't always allocated the genders to blue and pink the way we do today. A very adamant 1893 *New York Times* style piece titled "Finery for Infants" references the then-common assignment of pink as *obviously* a boy's color.

Together, the mom and her son used the manual yarn winder on the coffee table to turn each skein into a tidy ball. As I watched them, I thought more about colors.

I was tempted to choose something bold like the boy had, but eventually decided I wanted something neutral for an everyday item like a sleep suit.

Fiona put the colorful options back. We considered: Gray or brown? What about cream? Would dark gray be too much? Okay then, how about a light, light brown—a color that would (somewhat) hide stains but still felt like it popped with brightness. Yes, that was it, we agreed.

Next up: buttons. Fiona sweetly repeated the whole decision-making process for the five required buttons. We landed on medium-brown wooden buttons that would stand out against the light brown alpaca yarn but not too much.

Fiona had packed a seltzer and a snack for me, knowing that even without being pregnant, I typically need ample hydration and feeding. The first trimester had only ramped that up. I was constantly nauseated, bone-deep tired, and on the verge of passing out from low blood sugar.

Once I was snacking and happy with my yarn choices, Fiona started shopping for herself. She browsed the sample sweaters and tried on many. Seeing a sweater sketched out or even finished in a photo is one thing; seeing how it actually hangs on your body is another. Bruun Strik helpfully has a large mirror for this.

Fiona doesn't just browse, she documents. She takes notes. She takes photos. She tries on a sweater and immediately spots the design details she'd modify, many of which I hadn't noticed until she pointed them out.

After deciding on sweater patterns and yarn types, Fiona moved on to color. She stood in front of the mirror holding different skeins up to her face. Which ones washed her out? Which made her eyes pop?

About an hour later, with bags full of yarn, we left Bruun Strik. It felt like we were leaving with all their yarn, but really, we'd barely made a dent. Fiona carried everything to Hart Bageri down the street. There, she bought me a sandwich, a pastry, a latte, and another seltzer. Bellies full, she carried the yarn all the way back to our Airbnb, where I took a nap and she started knitting.

Sam kindly drove me to the San Francisco airport for my flight to Copenhagen, which coincided with heavy traffic time. So instead of spending forever idling in a car in bumper-to-bumper traffic, we decided to make a San Francisco day of it before dropping me off at the airport. For us, that means dumplings and books.

We stopped at Green Apple Books. It's been around since the sixties and feels like how a bookstore should—brimming with used and new books, all of which you want to read. The selection is eclectic but lovingly curated. Heart and thought have clearly gone into the selection. You might find the bestsellers here—but you might also not. You are just as likely to find some random academic press book as you are a bestseller.

I bought a book to read on the flight over, a recent work called *Natality* by Jennifer Banks. Banks is an editor at Yale University Press and a mother of three. In reading through book proposals, she came across this philosophy she'd never heard of before: natality.

Natality, Hannah Arendt's philosophy about birth, is the concept that we may not all be birthing people, but we are all birthed. As Banks writes, natality is the counterpoint to our societal emphasis on mortality. Arendt wrote about it in her 1958 book *The Human Condition*. In that book, Arendt (who didn't have children) argued that because we were once born, we can always begin again.

Best known for her writings on totalitarianism, Arendt was a prominent philosopher who escaped Nazi Germany in the 1930s. Based in New York for much of her life, she wrote about how we humans influence each other in good and bad ways; we live together with each other.

Arendt saw totalitarianism (in Nazism and Stalinism) as new and distinct from anything that had come before. It wasn't just extreme violence rained down from above or a one-off bad individual leading a government. Totalitarianism is an evilness that permeates everything and every level of a society, an ideology and terror conflated into the same thing that seeks to erase individuality, spontaneity, and plurality.

Totalitarianism thrives in social and political voids. Where traditional institutions aren't strong. Where loneliness runs rampant. Where ideology replaces truth. People turn to these violent existences to fill their voids, to have meaning and belonging and order. Sure, maybe some already had evil hatred inside of them. But most don't.

That's the scariest part. The awfulness that totalitarianism spreads often comes from shockingly mundane places—the banality of evil, as Arendt wrote.

For Arendt, our hope against totalitarianism lies in natality: We were born, we can always choose to begin again. We have a capacity to create, to be diverse, to be spontaneous, to be together. To live in a world not full of totalitarianism's voids but instead of alive hope, we must celebrate all that makes us human, starting with the fact that all of us were once born.

The philosophy of natality floored Banks so much, she ended up writing a book about the way in which Western society thinks of (and ignores) birth as a way to better understand natality and the roles birth play in our lives.

Arendt's understanding of natality isn't pro-natalist or about reproductive politics. It's about creation, freedom, unpredictability, political responsibility, and seeing the possibilities in life. You were born, that is amazing, so go live—and keep living (keep becoming).

As Banks writes, "We may die alone but we were never born alone." Inherent in the philosophy of natality is this theme of community and reliance on others. We are only ever always in the world with other people who are also constantly becoming.

This birth-forward philosophy seems to me a much better way of looking at the world than the currently overhyped trend surrounding stoic philosophy, where death infects your every decision. Memento mori—remember you must die—tells you to live now while you can. Sure, this perspective is intended to inspire gratitude for what you already have, provide immersion in the present, and free you from a fear of death. But it also feels like a philosophy with an underlying concern of holding tightly to what little you have left. Always be thinking about the ending.

Stoicism seems like a bummer to me. A small way to look at the world. A scarcity mindset, as they say.

Arendt's natality provides possibility—again and again. Each of us were once birthed. Because of that fact we can always begin again.

This, Arendt argues, gives you the freedom to start something, to create something new. But that freedom comes with responsibility and an understanding that you are acting in a world filled with others. That your actions have repercussions (good and bad). You may be able to begin again, but you can't necessarily undo what you start or its repercussions.

Today we might interpret that as a call for individual transformation—to read some self-help and go to therapy. Arendt saw natality as both public and relational: to be born means to join a world populated by others. We begin again by participating in the world among others also doing things in the world—a plurality to be celebrated.

I mean, that's what we all want, right? To feel fully alive in a world filled with others also doing the same. It was hard not to think about Arendt's emphasis on creativity and community as I walked around Copenhagen with Fiona.

At the end of our weeklong sister trip, Fiona headed to the airport and I to the train station. Fiona had packed her own bag full of yarn—and made sure mine was stuffed with seltzer and gummy bears as well as yarn. I wasn't yet done with my time in Denmark.

Back when I first met Marianne Isager (the Queen of Danish Knitting) at her knitting workshop in Fukuoka, she had invited me to visit her in Tversted, a tiny town in the far north of Denmark where her globally renowned yarn company, Isager Yarn, is headquartered.

I said yes right away—and then got even more excited when I realized the timing could line up perfectly with my Fiona trip. Later I learned that the week I was invited to visit also happened to be when some of Denmark's top knitwear designers would be gathering there for a weeklong summer vacation at Isager Yarn's headquarters. Yes, I could absolutely find a way to get myself to Tversted that week.

As I sat on a number of trains for the six-hour journey from Copenhagen to Tversted, I alternated between reading more of Jennifer Banks's book and knitting my Sailor Sweater from Isager yarns. Staring out the train window, watching the view become increasingly rural, I marveled at the fact that Marianne had not only created a powerhouse of design that sells yarn and knitwear designs on five continents, but she was doing so in a tiny town in northern Denmark, a surprisingly long way from Copenhagen.

Chapter 6

Hygge

Isager Yarn sells twenty-four different types of yarns—spanning everything from regular sheep wool to alpaca, baby alpaca, cotton, goat, specialty wools, and many blends of these fibers, each coming in dozens of colors. The colors tend to be earthy and deep—in everything from yellow to purple to gray. Nature, specifically the rural, oceanside nature of Tversted, heavily influences the color scheme.

Tversted looks like what you probably imagine for the rural Danish countryside: beautiful but muted landscapes, lots of open fields, minimalist architecture houses nestled into the landscape (and not too close to one another), a cold, sandy beach with waters that look both intriguing for their calm and terrifying for their chilly temperatures, and a sun that almost never rises in the winter and seems to never set in the summer. When the summer tourists leave, there are only 544 people left.

My first immersion into Tversted was literally that—a dip into the very cold North Sea. I arrived in the evening and early the next morning, Marianne Isager brought me with her to a daily Tversted tradition: a morning dip.

It felt Danish in a distinctly foreign way. Almost everyone besides us who showed up for the 8 a.m. swim was buck naked and over sixty. After an hour of floating and chatting in frigid water, everyone got out (and somewhat got dressed) for shots of homemade schnapps on the beach. Then someone with a camera corralled the group of fifty or so for the daily group swim photo. All of this on a Monday morning!

These are the same people you can count on to show up for a sing-along at 9 a.m. on Friday. Every Friday morning the Isager company's dining hall table is laden with free breakfast treats and strong coffee, and the room fills with townspeople. Together these folks enthusiastically (and loudly and sometimes very off-key) sing Danish songs. Then they chat, eat, and drink. I've never been so quickly passed by so many surprisingly fast-walking sixty-plus-year-olds as I was that Friday morning as I sleepily meandered over to breakfast after a few hours of jetlagged sleep under the bright midnight sun. They hustled past me like kids heading to recess.

Honestly, that's the best way to describe the enthusiasm Marianne brings and cultivates through Isager Yarn. It's about yarn, yes, but it's also about being together and doing things for the sake of doing them.

Everyone seemed to know Marianne and truly enjoyed her company. Marianne, a sixty-nine-year-old native of northern Denmark, moved her company to Tversted in 1980. Since then, she and the company have been intertwined in this interesting growth.

Basically, Tversted is a normal sleepy, aging beach town—except for the fact that it is also a crafting mecca and a hotspot of the knitting world. Isager Yarn took over the town's shuttered schoolhouse and turned it into a warehouse, offices, a cafe and playground open to the public, a store selling every kind of Isager yarn imaginable, bedrooms for guests (like me and the knitwear designers), artist studios for those tangentially (or not at all) related to the company, and a large, well-lit dining hall.

Marianne was just twenty-three when she inherited the yarn company. She was an art student in Aarhus, Denmark, under the mentorship of the company's founder, Åse Lund Jensen, who was a pioneer in the knitwear world but died unexpectedly young from cancer in 1977.

With her baby, Helga, on her hip, Marianne took over Åse's company. She took the best part of the tiny (a special but still quite niche) Danish yarn company—the quality of the yarn, the color schemes used, the artistic sensibilities of the patterns using the yarn—and expanded it, mostly through word of mouth, into its current world-renowned iteration. Forty years later, this company still has its corporate soul intact.

How did Isager Yarn become so successful? Everyone I asked talked about the people. They hire good people. They do joint ventures with good people. They treat people well, regardless of their status. They treat their distributors well, developing in-person friendships with those who farm, manufacture, and sell their yarn. They hold workshops for their excitable customers—and geek out with them over playing with yarn. (There's a yoga and knitting workshop held annually in Tversted that sounds extremely relaxing.) They curate gatherings of kind, interesting people.

The weeklong vacation Marianne had invited me to was one of these gatherings. Her company invited the top Danish knitwear designers and any interested family members to relax, hang out, and enjoy each other's company and the Tversted summertime. Everyone understood that sure, there is a significant business interest in having top designers suggest to their customers to use Isager yarn for projects and for the designers to be in the favor of such a well-established yarn company. But it never felt like a purely transactional visit.

I found myself in an Alice in Wonderland alternate universe where everyone cares deeply about community and knitting, a combination that translated into an inhabited real-life hygge. I had always figured that hygge, like a lot of trends written in absolutes (*X country always does Y*), was a load of overhyped marketing by Americans desperately wishing life in other countries was lived better than how we do it. Turns out, I was wrong. Hygge is real. It's alive and well—and very dimly lit and cozy.

I showed up to Tversted with a lot of yarn from the Copenhagen shops and my half-done Sailor Sweater. It was a good thing I had a knitting project, because in the evenings the designers would all knit.

We'd gather in a room that looked like the most physical embodiment of real-life hygge I've ever seen: dim, multitiered lighting, ample ingredients to make an array of warm drinks, a record player spinning everything from ABBA to Miles Davis, and cozy couches and chairs arranged in a circle to sink into, knit, and chat.

Lining the room were sweaters piled up neatly in glass cases. They're the samples of the patterns Marianne has designed over the last forty years. Sprinkled among the sweaters in the cases are her many self-published books on knitting.

Above the cases hung large, artistic posters of important knitting techniques—the old-school drawing version of tutorials before YouTube came along and let you watch (and rewatch twenty more times) the hands of strangers demonstrating knitting skills, the hands that taught me how to start a sweater at the beginning of the pandemic.

With me in this hygge room were five designers: Anne Ventzel (@AnneVentzel), whose designs, like my Sailor Sweater, give knitters a structured colorwork design in which they can experiment; Mette Wendleboe Okkels (@PetiteKnit), the Instagram-famous designer whose accessible patterns come from a deep grasp of math; Maja Klovdal (@OtherLoops), who crafts in three dimensions with soft, flowing features; and Helga Jona (@HelgaJona), whose patterns play with intricate texture. Managing it all was Helga Isager (@HelgaIsager), Marianne's daughter and co-runner of the company. Helga wears many hats at Isager, including the popular collaborative design rollouts where Isager provides the style guidelines and the top knitwear designers craft a sweater for one specific collection.

Working on the Sailor Sweater next to the woman who designed the pattern would have been incredibly intimidating had Anne Ventzel not been so kind. As we knit during the evenings, she worked on creating new patterns and we chatted about color choices and life.

Through her pattern, Anne had already taught me new knitting skills. The Sailor Sweater's neck is subtly boat-shaped, not the usual round hole you'd find in a sweater. Achieving that shape required that I learn new ways of approaching purl and knit knots—and then somewhat sliding them around on my needles in ways I would never have considered without Anne's instructions.

The look of the sweater also comes from the type of yarn Anne suggests you use. It's two types of Isager yarn that you hold together while you knit them as a single strand. The pairing of hardy Jensen sheep wool and delicate Alpaca gives the sweater a thin, fine, and extremely soft feel while still being quite sturdy and warm.

Having to hold two strands of yarn also means you get to subtly expand the colors of your sweater. You get to pick four colors—two for the stripe and two for the base. Holding a sturdy and a fine yarn at the same time while knitting is a pretty common trick, but most of the time knitters choose the same color for those two strands. Companies like Isager make sure their color schemes match across all their yarns for this very purpose.

I like to play with color more than that. If you pick similar-ish colors, say a medium gray and a dusty dark blue, you get to create your own color. They mix together like watercolors—the colors blending as if they were liquids, not solids. You get this magic trick because the fine yarn is so thin compared to the heft of the sturdier yarn. If you hold two thick yarns together—or two opposing colors—you instead get speckles of discrete color.

I learned this trick not by choice but because American yarn shops usually have much smaller stock options than do their Danish counterparts. Tversted lets you get creative in the opposite direction. Isager has two yarn shops in the tiny town. One is almost a learning place with its home-grown dyes, and the other is a place where you could roll around in yarns forever in every color imaginable.

These women had always been knitting. Their mothers knit. Their grandmothers knit. They knit with their friends. To them, it has always been popular. But nowadays other people do it too. As we talked and knit, I couldn't help but look around at the scene I found myself in. We, a group of kind, interesting women, were spending the evening chatting and making things in a cozy room with jazz playing—all because of knitting. Yes, it's all those big issues (fast fashion, individual creativity, etc.) of *why* knitting. It's also just this—it's an engaging activity that works as a solo and a relatively low-key communal activity. It's an excuse for women to get together and have fun. That's the magic of knitting.

Women in Denmark have been making things with wool—often in communal settings—for a really long time. Back in the Bronze Age in Denmark, way before even the Vikings, women were using sheep wool for weaving, felting, and nalbinding.

Nalbinding is this yarn technique that seems almost the same as knitting except for a few expert-level differences. You take spun yarn, your fingers, and *one* needle and chain loop the yarn a bunch of times to form a larger textile. Knitting does the same, except it is a series of knots and made using *two* needles. It doesn't show up in the European historical record until the medieval period. With traders, knitting traveled from the Middle East into Spain and then the rest of Europe.

Woolen textiles made the Vikings the fierce explorers, raiders, colonizers, and traders that they were. Sails and most clothes were wool. They expanded their Scandinavian empire both for the thrills of conquering and for the very real needs of sheep: The more the Vikings conquered, the more wool they needed to keep the whole production running, and the more land they needed for sheep to graze. Once you give a mouse a cookie, he'll demand more wool.

Women so dominated the Vikings' textile field in an otherwise deeply patriarchal society that it terrified the men. I really mean terrified. There are all these poems and myths about how men should leave women working on textiles the fuck alone on pain of death. For example, myths about female Viking deities using the skulls of men as loom weights to foretell which men were going to die in an upcoming battle. You know, real casual.

Women crafted, chatted, and built their communities in women-only houses called *dyngja* where they created their textiles. Women's magic and power were often linked with textile production—the women were seen to be literally spinning the world into existence and cutting the threads of life. To mess with that was to risk mystical danger and the main source keeping the Viking economy turning.

Textiles in medieval Scandinavia became intricately linked to the economy in even more explicit ways than before, when the Viking women textiles heavily carried the economy. Now, in the medieval period, textiles basically were the economy, used as we use cash—and women still largely controlled textiles, including sometimes being the sellers of the textiles.

Eventually women in Denmark lost that power and somewhere along the way, men took over textiles. It was a slow slide, at first, but had dramatically happened by the time the Industrial Revolution had machines spitting out mass-produced textiles (with the help of underpaid women and child labor). That occurred as Europe regressed into the awful, disempowered gender stereotypes of the seventeenth through twentieth centuries. Somewhere along the way, women lost the power they had held with textiles.

By the nineteenth century in Denmark, you still have women hand-knitting, but mostly alone, at night, making clothes for their immediate family members. There isn't the allure of the terrifying magic of women producing textiles together in women-only spaces, like the Viking women enjoyed. Or the high prices that medieval women could fetch for their work. Instead, you find women and girls (and some poor men—oh the indignity!) knitting in the evening, often begrudgingly and certainly not for pleasure or power.

By the time Åse Lund Jensen (Marianne's mentor) showed up on the Danish scene in the early twentieth century, knitting was a dreary task of making ugly, ill-fitting clothes for warmth because you're too poor to buy fashionable store-sold ones. Åse changed all that.

Like with most good innovations, annoyance helped. Åse was annoyed at only being able to buy knitting yarn in drab colors—when much better colors were available for "artistic" textile work like weaving. Weaving, a supposedly "real" art that was displayed on walls, not bodies, deserved good colors and legitimate artistic appreciation.

Åse was sure that hand-knitting was a beautiful art deserving of quality supplies and attention from the artistic (read: mostly male) field. When her application for membership, as a knitwear designer, into Den Permanente (a Danish crafts cooperative for artists) was rejected—because the colors of her knitting were "not satisfactory" (read: ugly)—Åse set about changing things.

She got a high-quality mill, Henrichsen's Wool Mill, to produce fine yarn and dye it in beautiful colors—synthetic dyes inspired by natural dye colors, so that they'd last longer but still be pretty. She set about making better patterns—ones that looked tailored to women's bodies with attention to details that you'd find in high-quality clothing.

Throughout all of this, Åse's focus was on hand knitting, not machine knitting, which was the way most cheap sweaters were made then and today. As she said, "Oh yes, one can even knit patterns on those apparatuses, and it looks really nice—just like false teeth."

Åse, like every good trailblazing woman, opened up some major doors for those who have come after. She opened the door for women like Marianne, who opened it for women like Mette.

Mette's innovation was to make knitting accessible. She purposely designs sweater patterns beginners can do—and want to wear afterward. All of her patterns are accompanied by how-to tutorial videos, featuring the hands and narration of her friend Kimmie Munkholm. I, like many women, learned how to make increasingly more difficult sweaters by following Mette's instructions and Kimmie's videos.

Åse and Marianne made sure the yarn was high quality and the patterns artistically tailored. Mette and Kimmie ensured we could all make beautiful sweaters. The other designers, like Helga Isager, Helga Jona, Maja Klovdal, and Anne Ventzel, gave us beautiful options to creatively play with technique and colors. All of these women are making a decent living off of their knitting contributions. It seems, to me, like the ideal of women's work—a feminist capitalistic dreamscape powered by colorful soft yarn and Instagram.

People think of knitting as mindless, but what I was finding was that it was incredibly mind-intensive. Until I really started knitting more seriously, I never realized how much math—mostly geometry and algebra—goes into it, even with swatches. It's way more than counting stitches.

A sweater, like all clothes, is shapes put together. How you mash together those shapes requires geometry—from how the sleeve hits the sweater's body to turning a 2D sketch into a 3D object. If you want to vary anything about the sweater design once you start knitting it, you'll have to get into some serious math.

Want to make the sweater slightly larger but not the next size up? You'll need some algebra to figure out how a few increases around the neckline are going to have cascading effects farther down the sweater as it smoothly widens down to the parts that hit your hips.

Want to make the stripes different colors, say, a rainbow? How many balls of yarn should you buy in each color? The red at the neckline is going to need a lot less yarn than the purple of the hips, especially if you want sleeve stripes to match the body. If you do your calculations wrong, you risk buying too much yarn. Or worse, too little—and then risk the yarn shop having run out of that specific indigo, forcing you to use a slightly different color of yarn and embrace your math mistake as part of the creative process.

The more I watched these women knit, the more I appreciated that they were math geniuses. It was impressive how quickly they could calculate what any alteration could mean to the number of stitches and amount of yarn needed.

Like most knitters, they began with the building blocks of every sweater, small ten-by-ten-centimeter squares called swatches. These small squares let them see how the yarn looks knitted up—sometimes it turns out quite differently than it looks wound up. These squares also let them mix together colors, like I do with the multiple colors held together as one yarn thread, or as stripes or spots or other shapes against a different-colored backdrop.

Swatches even let you try out textures: How do cables look in this yarn? What about bobbles? Small bobbles? Big bobbles?

I'm not yet able to design my own sweaters, but I find that even while following another's pattern, I can still relish the creativity and originality involved. Even a simple knit stitch requires creative thinking. Humans have been playing with knots for a long time. New knots are still being invented all the time. You can knit a stitch on a sweater through several processes, many of which will result in the same end result. But how you get to that outcome depends on your preferences and who taught you how to knit—in person or through their patterns.

I like that we all have to make swatches, from the earliest beginners to the biggest experts. That the first step—a swatch—in making any sweater is learning how to start to see the full sweater from just a piece, like a designer does.

You knit up a swatch to see if your knitting style and yarn choice are relatively similar to what the designer imagined. If she got twenty-six stitches by eighteen stitches for her ten-centimeter squared swatch—and you did too—then you're good to go. If not, you're gonna need to make some adjustments (different needle size or yarn or something) or you'll risk making a wildly different-sized sweater.

I thought about this math as we knit together. The designers made their swatches—and quietly did color, fiber, and math calculations—and I followed Anne's pattern, working on the hem of the sweater's body. Helga Isager was playing with stripes of differing colors against a cream background, all in yarn so incredibly soft that you could put it next to a baby's skin. Anne was pairing colors that in balled-up form seemed like they'd clash horribly, but knitted up magically complemented each other. Mette was playing with texture, creating dimension and thickness in her swatches.

Mette told me that she purposely designs her sweaters to put the knitter in different types of flow states—either the ease of many knit stitches leading you into a hazy meditative repetitive state or a complicated pattern that requires hyper focus on every stitch in the immediate now. On this night, the mood was calm, a bit sleepy from the rain, and playful, our own little modern *dyngja*.

When I casually mentioned to a few of the knitwear designers about how feminist I thought this ideal women's work landscape seemed, they politely told me to go fuck myself. Wait, what?

I was so confused. What they were doing made them seem like some of the most feminist women I had ever met. They support each other and other women. They run their own companies, employ other women. They are all the primary earners of their families. They're raising wonderful children, whom they seem to cherish, but they don't let that dominate their entire existence. They're carving out economic spheres for themselves and other women by taking a historically confining thing and turning it into an empowering, artistic endeavor.

Archaeologist Michèle Hayeur Smith has written a book about Danish and Icelandic medieval women and textiles, *The Valkyries' Loom: The Archaeology of Cloth Production and Female Power in the North Atlantic*. And to me one of the most fascinating things is why she wrote it—for her daughter: "As a member of the next generation of women fighting for equal rights," Hayeur Smith writes, "she and her peers need to know where we came from and what we accomplished in the past. This knowledge can only make them stronger and help them forge their own definition of gender equality based on female ways and female power rather than defining their equality by comparing themselves to men."

All of the knitwear designers but Mette told me they weren't feminists. They liked men, they explained, and having partners. Or, they'd say, using feminism as a lens is reductive of people to their genders. They preferred to be understood as people who knitted (and happened to be women) and sold knitting patterns (to *mostly* people who happened to be women).

My feeble response that the personal is political, and that I'm a feminist who also doesn't hate men, was politely not really heard. They entertained my questions, but still didn't agree that they were doing feminist work—just interesting, good, profitable work.

But I had concocted an entire narrative about what women's work means—and here was a roomful of strong, interesting women doing it! Was this me being an American and imposing my values onto them? Were they right that feminism had been "solved in the 1970s," as one Danish woman in Copenhagen had told me, and that bringing it up actually created further divides between the sexes? Instead, should I be seeing these knitwear designers as humans who *happened* to be women and who *happened* to work in a field of almost exclusively women and *happened* to sell mostly to women and *happened* to be building on a tradition that women have historically dominated for generations and is currently seen as almost exclusively female?

The knitwear designers live in a country that reads to my American sensibilities as very feminist: great work-life balance, good workplace rights, amazing childcare, guaranteed maternity and paternity leave, and a general equality vibe.

But only one in six Danes consider themselves feminist. Denmark is a pretty conformist country—asking any of them to say loudly that they disagree hits them about the same way as asking an American to go burn a bra. Basically, a radical act that will garner you some side-eyes at best. The old in-your-face, fuck-all-men 1960s feminism is how most Danes understand the term today. When questioned (by yours truly or in country-wide polls), most Danes are for equality among the genders—my American definition of modern-day feminism.

By calling something women's work, I'm not trying to say that textiles can only be created by women or that women can't do other types of work. I'm trying to say: Hey, this thing that seems dominated by women—at least over the last few centuries—used to seem like a super bummer of a dreary task that women couldn't escape from. But in different periods of history, including now, women have instead turned textile work into an option that allows them to have a lot of freedom and power.

Really, that's what I want to get at by looking at work done primarily by women today—what is it that makes this work interesting and special, and how does that work let these women live their lives however they want? That last bit, by the way, is how I'd define an empowered woman. I'm pretty sure the Danes would agree with me on that.

The designers had brought some of their families with them for this holiday week: a few spouses and almost all their children. The kids were given pretty free range to go play. Throughout the day you could hear the joyful shouts of the children in the distance.

The summer night sunlight shined bright. Denmark is far far north, and in Tversted the sun wouldn't start setting until around 10:30 and was up again by 4 a.m.

All of us, kids and adults, had eaten at maybe 5:30 p.m. but hours later, the sky looked no different—a bright blue. We sat at picnic benches pulled together to make one long makeshift dinner table. The knitwear designers had prepared salads, breads, fish, and potatoes. (Danes love potatoes.) Supposedly these were dishes the designers had "just thrown together," but they looked Noma-like and worthy of the Instagram photos that then turned up on the internet later, highlighting our dinners. Clearly it wasn't just me who thought these dinners were idyllic.

It was performative, sure. But honestly, after a few well-curated snaps, the phones went away, and the conversation lingered for hours. This was every night during our weeklong vacation. Though sometimes we sat at long tables inside.

The wine flowed. Tiny wine glasses were constantly being filled for each other. A variation of reds and whites for them. Juice, nicely, for me.

The conversation would start in English but often wandered back into Danish. Most Danes, while fluent in

English, are much more comfortable in their native language. Add that to the collectivist nature of the country—being thoughtful enough to speak the language the majority of the group is comfortable in—and you've got a slightly tipsy conversation spoken largely in Danish.

I didn't mind. It let me zone out and take in my surroundings.

An occasional kid would wander over. Sit in a lap for some minutes and then leave to go explore. They'd be welcomed, included in the conversation, and then let go on their way when they got bored of the adults. No yelling. No micro-managing. No chicken nuggets. An occasional kid meltdown or fight, sure. But those, too, were handled with gentle serenity.

As I sat there, half-listening to Danish I couldn't understand, I spent time watching birds fly around, catching the insects that hopped around our feet in the grass.

Eventually, one of the knitwear designers would notice that I'd been staring at a nearby tree for nearly twenty minutes and would shift the conversation back into English for my benefit. We talked rowing, swimming, running, and the other sports some of us did.

Travel came up, excitement about upcoming trips and reminiscing about places many of us had been. Isager Yarn does a lot of business in Japan. Marianne and her husband lived part-time in Tokyo for many years. Helga Isager has traveled throughout Japan a bunch of times. She told me about bringing her young daughter with her on a work trip to Japan.

Just the two of them. It wasn't necessarily the easiest, but it was great, she said.

Maja told me how kids make travel even more fun. How traveling by camper van is a great way to adventure with little ones because then they have the same bed even as the location changes.

Again and again, they reiterated: Both halves of the title "working mother" add fun dimensions to their lives. Life doesn't stop because you have kids. It gets richer. It gets deeper.

These weren't platitudes either. As the conversation switched back into Danish, I looked around where I was: at one of the most northern tips of Denmark surrounded by the most idyllic creative motherhood scene. It wasn't a fantasy or a projection of how life should be. It was a gathering of women unassumingly adamant that creativity, motherhood, working, and friendship obviously go together.

It reminded me of a term I had learned while reading Jennifer Banks's book *Natality*: matrescence. Based on the word adolescence, it was created in 1973 by medical anthropologist Dana Raphael as a way to represent how motherhood is an ongoing process. Just as teenagers don't become functioning adults overnight just because the hormones have started, neither do women become fully functioning mothers just because they pop out a baby. It's a process. Usually a pretty ungainly one. Both teenagers and mothers look to outsiders as if they have it together much more than they feel they do on the inside. Teens are literally children in the bodies of adults: basically the cartoon of three raccoons stacked up in a trench coat.

Just as we're constantly becoming adults and growing into ourselves, even after we're twenty-five, so too are mothers. Sure, some of the biggest changes happen in the nine months leading up to birth and the nine months post-birth. But, as Raphael wrote into the concept of matrescence, that motherhood learning process never stops. As your child goes through different life stages, so do you as a mother to them. Parenting a four-year-old is wildly different than parenting a fourteen-year-old.

I sat a lot during my time in Tversted. There were nice places to walk, like the beach, but I physically couldn't do it with my first-trimester nausea and fatigue. So instead I hung around the school turned yarn shop and knitting mecca and finished reading Banks's book.

Honestly, reading about matrescence really helped me chill out about the idea of becoming a mother. If it's a process, then I can learn and take things as they come. If it's a switch flip, well then I have a ton more research to do: I have no idea how to potty train yet. I don't even know what books to start reading. That's okay. I'll get to it in due time.

So it was useful to think about matrescence, since I was in the beginning stages. But I wasn't ready to think about motherhood or postpartum or teenage years yet. I was still in the pregnancy, the creation phase of my motherhood journey.

Part II

Doing

Chapter 7

Precarity

While I had been knitting under the midnight sun, Sam had set up our rental house in Berkeley. It had a blue door that faced toward a small roundabout through which parents biked their kids to school. Giant oak trees lined the street, down which we could walk to coffee shops and nearby parks.

With my focus on Japan and admiration of the Danish knitters, I had perhaps discounted the explosion of craft going on back home in the United States. The Bay Area has an abundance of creativity. I couldn't figure out why I had resisted living here for so long. Here were tech nerds who played outside and crafted. Women were knitting in cafes alongside the many remote workers on laptops, wearing clothes that looked distinctly homemade. People displayed their handmade ceramics at home, and they were out in droves hiking, biking, and sea foraging.

I seized on sea foraging as the first creative practice to try out in the Bay Area. Sure, I could have equally gone with sewing or knitting, but I wanted to move my body. It was the beginning of summer, and I wanted to be outside. At night I'd put on a history audiobook and keep working on my Sailor Sweater. But during the daytime, I wanted sunshine.

I knew from my time with the ama that sea foraging could be many things—and that given the Pacific was the same ocean, what Bay Area folks were after would be similar to what the ama foraged. I knew from the ama that seasonality really mattered. Right time and place will give you abundance without hurting the overall ecosystem. Harvest something in the wrong season, and you'll be hurting next year's abundance.

That made sense for mussels, sea urchin, abalone, and all the other shellfish the ama foraged, but I hadn't thought about it when seeing the seaweed drying on racks outside ama huts. I kinda had just figured that seaweed was like grass—a background thing, not something to be foraged. I hadn't thought to ask the ama about it. Seaweed is ubiquitous in Japan: in soups, around sushi, as side dishes, and in fancy lotions. I hadn't thought about its life cycle or how one might sustainably forage it.

As I started looking into my options for sea foraging in the Bay Area, I kept coming across notices about seaweed foraging. It turned out that not only does one forage for seaweed in similar ways one might go looking for sea urchin, but that I had shown up in the Bay Area at exactly the right season—summertime.

It felt kismet: right time, right place, lots of like-minded people. I figured I'd start with seaweed and then work my way up to bigger, more adventurous sea foraging.

I've always loved seaweed. As kids we'd have it as an afternoon snack, eating just sheets of it or crumbling it onto popcorn. I'd devour sushi anytime and all the time, loving the juxtaposition of the crunch of dried seaweed against the plump rice and smooth fish. My mom always added it into any pot of beans to reduce gas. But I never gave it much thought. I figured seaweed was seaweed—I was in my twenties before I realized that there were hundreds of types.

The Bay Area's coast alone has 300-something varieties of seaweed. There's kombu (what my mom put into a pot of beans) and nori (which is wrapped around sushi). But there's also bladderwrack, which has such high levels of iron that eating it could replace an iron supplement. There's cystoseira, which works great as a pickled dish. There's cat's tongue, which you can use as an exfoliant and moisturizer in your bath. That's not to mention the many cookbooks devoted to helping you figure out other ways to include seaweed in your meals. Put it in sushi! Add it to your fish dish! Steam this one. Sprinkle that one onto pasta.

All of this is just outside your door in the Bay Area. Pop down to the beach, harvest some seaweed, dry it, and eat it. My visions of being a California lady of nature who could forage like the ama with friends and then go work on my Danish sweater at night seemed to be easily coming to fruition. I was going to be one of those mothers who grabs some produce from my garden, some mussels and seaweed from the nearby beach, and a loaf of sourdough from the nearby world-renowned bakery and whips together a delicious feast that we'd eat outside around a table covered with a linen tablecloth, pleasantly mismatched silverware, and porcelain plates. There'd probably even be a jug of fresh lemonade from a neighbor's tree. Maybe these neighbor-friends would even join us for this quickly thrown-together meal.

I figured all I needed to do to make that vision come true was learn how to seaweed forage. Early in my first trimester, my thoughts of nesting were less about setting up a nursery than about giving my kid a life of adventure. (Perhaps not the most practical, and yet here we are.) I wanted to be this creative lady of nature who forages and teaches my future kid how to do it.

I found a seaweed-foraging class (they seemingly have classes for everything in the Bay Area) and got a friend to come with me. When I'm looking to do something adventurous and silly but also intentional, I know I can count on my friend Sophie.

I've known her for over a decade, since our early graduate school days. Add Sophie and you're probably going to have a good time—be it her ability to quote most female rappers, posit about French existential philosophy, deeply listen, dive deep into a wonky policy discussion, give a piercing side-eye with a smile when you've said something dumb, and crack a perfectly timed joke. She will also wake up at the crack of dawn for something worthwhile.

We made a long weekend out of the seaweed-foraging trip with our partners, Sam and McLean. The four of us drove up the coast—stopping for some fresh sourdough bread at possibly the best bread bakery in the Bay Area, Wild Flour Bread. Sophie found us a campsite along the Russian River that was sheltered and quiet but not far from where we'd go foraging the next morning.

While the guys slept in, Sophie and I woke up at 4:30 a.m. and drove ten minutes to the beach. There we met up with Heidi Herrmann, our instructor. Heidi knows what she's doing. As the owner of Strong Arm Farm, she sells wild foraged Sonoma Coast seaweed to local restaurants and grows organic perennial flowers. She gave off strong ama vibes— you could quickly tell she was someone happiest near the ocean. She's got sun-bleached blonde hair and smile wrinkles, teaches native plant classes at Santa Rosa Junior College, and had gardening shears at the ready to quickly demonstrate how to cut fresh seaweed as she bounded around the tidal pools spouting seaweed facts.

With us were two other Bay Area women who had made the ninety-minute drive up to the beach in Sonoma that morning in a share car—the kind you unlock with an app. With no cell phone service, they had to leave the car doors open the whole time we were seaweed foraging so they could access the car to drive back to Berkeley.

No one else was at the beach other than the five of us. It had that ama feel—of athletic women on an empty, quiet beach being in touch with nature. We got there as the sun was rising. We scrambled around the tidal rocks and learned to recognize all the different types of seaweed.

Directed by Heidi, we put handfuls of it in plastic bags. She'd point you to a variety, say kombu, and tell you where to cut it (at the stem, almost like a flower). After we all had some of that type, she'd bring us to a different area of the tidal zone and point out a completely different seaweed, like the almost twig-like brown-green bladderwrack (the type that could theoretically replace my daily iron supplement), and tell us how and where to cut off a handful. Next, it was cat's tongue hiding among rocks—Heidi was incredibly enthusiastic about how wonderful this was as a bath-time exfoliant, explaining that she gave so much of it to her niece for multiple years that her niece requested other presents for next Christmas.

As we waded around the tidal pools looking under and around rocks, Heidi explained that seaweed foraging has a shortish window here in the Bay Area. Mostly, it's summer. And you want to hit it at low tide. If you can show up to a tidal pool at super-low tides, that'll make it even easier to harvest seaweed.

Of course, there's seaweed year-round, but you don't want to harvest them when they're spawning. Yeah, you read that right—seaweed spawn. They release spores out into the ocean, letting the currents determine the fate of their offspring. You want to keep the seaweed generations going and so foragers avoid harvesting when it's spawning time. Plus, spawning seaweed doesn't taste that good.

Outside of spawning time, there's still much of the year that isn't good for harvesting seaweed. It's there, but there's far less of it—and what you do find will be kinda ratty and not in fresh shape. Likely most of it will be stuff you find washed up on shore—a big no-no in seaweed harvesting. Heidi emphasized that you only harvest growing seaweed. Anything that is washed up on the beach might make you sick.

As we were leaving, Heidi let us know that you need to get your seaweed home for drying relatively quickly after harvesting it. If you don't get it out of your plastic bags and drying in the sun, it'll rot quickly and your efforts will have been a waste.

It felt like opening a new avenue of play in nature here in the Bay Area. As we drove home, I felt all-in on foraging. I was ready to take a million different classes on harvesting and eating "native" plants. I didn't quite know what I'd do with my seaweed, but I felt confident I'd really get in touch with the sea this way—and be able to teach a future kid how to do so as well.

As we unpacked our gear, I put the bags of seaweed on the dining room table. I felt so proud of those ziplock bags, sure this bounty would be the first of many.

But then in almost the next moment, all of a sudden foraged things started to feel a bit scarier being pregnant. The excitement started to slide into a low hum of anxiety. I looked at the bags and started to ask questions I didn't know the answers to: What if there was something on the seaweed that made me sick? Was it really just me who was responsible for knowing if something I found out in nature was really safe? Isn't that what the FDA is for?

I wasn't ready to give up on my lady of nature vision just yet. Sophie and I had talked up seaweed foraging so much that Sam wanted to give it a try. He and I signed up for another class—this one, because of the tidal schedule, started on a weekday at 6 a.m. in Halfmoon Bay. Heidi wasn't the teacher for this class. This teacher, a kind woman, was a forager and herbalist.

Everything about the class was different. For one, it had a lot more people than the one Sophie and I had taken— perhaps because of the closer location or the slightly more palatable start time.

It felt like a class field trip gone wrong. There were far too many people for this teacher to monitor. While she was distracted helping one of the older members walk on the slick rocks, the rest of the class raced to pile seaweed into their plastic bags. People walked on top of seaweed. Other people then foraged that seaweed (while talking about how they weren't going to wash it, because that would rinse away the good nutrients in the seawater).

The class with Sophie had been slightly earlier in the season, so everything was in abundance. This crop was picked over—it was nearing the end of the harvesting season and at an easily accessed beach. In the previous class, we had all taken some, but not a lot of, seaweed. Now people seemed to hoard it.

I wasn't rushing around. I was tired, and nervous about slipping and falling—what if I landed weird on my stomach? I watched people step again and again on perfectly good seaweed and then didn't harvest that—and wondered what other seaweed I might harvest and if it had also been already stepped on.

I then started to think about coastal runoff—what sort of pollutants were washing off the roads and over-pesticided lawns (or worse!) and into the ocean right here. Sure, supposedly this beach was deemed "safe" for foraging—but what did that really mean? Was I being incredibly stupid and irresponsible as a pregnant person? And for what? Why was I really doing this?

On my dawn beach trip with Sophie, seaweed foraging had seemed deeply purposeful, as close as I could get to an ama-like lifestyle in the US. This just seemed dumb and performative. I started to spiral: It felt like we were racing through a grocery store.

I certainly didn't feel a oneness with the universe or more ecologically minded as I stood there on the beach with my small bag of seaweed I didn't know what I'd do with. I felt silly and small and hungry and tired. And worried that whatever was in that bag—was it safe to eat?

We went and ate a generic diner breakfast after the class—some fine-enough eggs and hash browns. Sam tried to cheer me up. That sucked but maybe it was just because it was a dumb class? We'd try it again. This time on our own—like real sea foragers, not just adult learners on a field trip.

I researched king tides (the biggest ones), the beaches where you're permitted to go, what you're allowed to harvest— all of the things. We again woke up early and drove to the coast. Upon arrival, we felt lucky to even get a parking spot. The lot was overflowing with Patagonia-bedecked foragers in Telsas, Priuses, Subarus, and pickup trucks. Clearly, the rest of the Bay Area had already gotten there before us.

We walked past big signs that specified what you could forage and when. A Fish and Wildlife warden checked everyone's catch as they left. He was quite busy—as we walked onto the beach, many people were already leaving, carrying bulging bags and overflowing buckets of shellfish and seaweed.

The tidal pools were picked over. We saw a few lonely sea stars and tiny snails too small to be harvested. I couldn't help but think about how abalone (the cash cow of the ama) used to be something you could easily harvest along the Bay Area coastline. Now it's heavily regulated, due to pressure on the species from overharvesting, ecosystem changes, and climate change.

Both in Japan and here in the Bay Area, there are rules about where you can go, in what season, and what individual species (and how much) you can harvest. But, in America—unlike Japan—there are not regulations about *who* is allowed to sea forage. The ama literally have permits to be ama. They can only go in certain areas for their individual sea foraging, places where other people can't go. As an American, I do think it's a nice thing that anyone can go sea foraging, but like many things, there are also downsides.

It's one of the nice things and bummers of the Bay Area. A lot of people here share interests similar to mine. It means I can easily make friends. It also means that a lot of people's ideas of a good weekend are the same as mine: time playing outside, maybe a hip coffee shop, waiting in line at a good bakery, eating at a delicious restaurant. Things get crowded quickly.

I just wasn't sure this whole seaweed-foraging thing was worth the effort if it meant being in big crowds of people also desperate for some kind of connection to nature. Especially if part of that connection was predicated on harvesting something from nature. It was starting to feel like, after researching the tides, knowing the regulations, waking up early, driving to a beach, and dealing with the crowds, all I was left with was a bit of seaweed that dried up into even smaller shriveled bits.

Later that day, I stood in our kitchen looking at my wet seaweed. I wondered aloud where in the pantry eventually to put the dried seaweed and what in the world I should cook to use it. Sam smiled at me and gently said, "You know you can just buy this at the grocery store?"

I wasn't ready to give up yet. I found another sea-foraging class for us, this one run by Kirk Lombard, the founder of Sea Forager—a CSA-like food subscription for sustainably harvested seafood. It was called the "San Francisco Coastal Fishing and Foraging Class." Here, I thought, at last would get us sea foraging the Bay Area like the ama.

It turns out I signed us up for being lectured at for three hours while we looked at the ocean, but didn't go in. We were told in theory how to do the things: what poles to use, how to create your own spears for stabbing eels hiding in rocks, how to catch crabs, how to cast different nets for herring season, how to scale the tiny herrings, and many other things. But since we didn't have fishing licenses (a requisite for many sea-foraging activities), the class was all theory, no practice. The closest we came to sea foraging was when we practiced throwing nets in the parking lot. For thirty minutes, we tried to catch imaginary fish.

More important, all the sea-foraging options the class laid out were distinctly unappealing. I don't like the taste of herring. The idea of stabbing eels grosses me out. Eating crab, even when someone else has caught, killed, and prepared it for you at a restaurant, always seems like a lot of work for not that much food.

The other options didn't fit with me being a pregnant lady. I wasn't going to collect mussels or really any shellfish that might be contaminated with red tide poisoning. Abalone wasn't an option.

I certainly wasn't going spearfishing pregnant. But also, to be fair, I probably wasn't going spearfishing before or after pregnancy—hunting is not my jam.

I could see how all of this, with the right perspective and motivation, fell squarely within the realm of cræft. Here was bodily wisdom that was deeply place- and tool-based. Casting nets for herring—even crafting the nets—required embodied knowledge only gained through repetition and learning from mentors.

I mean, I had even found the potential mentors! The sea foraging teachers were all kind and so eager to share their knowledge. It was all easily there for me to delve into this creative practice. I could have done the pregnancy-friendly parts of Bay Area sea foraging (seaweed harvesting, herring catching, etc.) while learning about the tides, the foraging spots, the government regulations. Then I'd be set to do bigger, more dramatic sea foraging once the baby was born.

The problem was: I didn't want to. I wasn't vibing with this type of creativity. I was starting to realize that what I had really liked about sea foraging with the ama was just the free-diving part. I didn't actually want to go poling for eels or throwing nets for herring.

I needed to expand my search.

I decided to try an obvious sea-adjacent creative practice: nature journaling. A Bay Area company, Wild Awake, ran classes teaching tidal pool nature journaling on the same beach where Sam and I had gone seaweed foraging by ourselves. I figured this would be a nice way to re-see the beach and ocean there. Maybe this was the calm, purposeful, sea-based creative practice I was after?

I got my friend Frances to join me. She can think circles around you about the most obscure policy-wonk topics but also is quick with a joke, can whip up the most amazing dishes, and has been known to casually practice her fly-fishing technique in abandoned grassy lots.

Nature journaling, I figured, is like going on an intentional hike with an emphasis on creativity. You deeply notice and creatively interact with a beautiful place.

I loved the idea of it—capture the curve of a shell, the sparkle of light on the waves, the depth of colors in sand. Nature journaling lets you deepen your interaction with a moment. Spend thirty minutes drawing a single shell and you'll remember its color tones much more vividly than if you step over it while walking on the beach—if you even see it.

I could picture myself in the future delighting in this creative practice. Maybe I wasn't going to harvest my own meals every week, but maybe I'd go foraging for things to draw. A catch-and-release kind of ama. I could be pregnant and easily enough sit on the beach and draw.

The goal of Wild Awake, the small company running the class, is to connect people with nature. To get them to creatively engage with the world around them. As they say in their tagline, "Awe is our antidote."

Their other events are even more Bay Area crunchy in their creativity and connection to nature: ocean sound baths, painting with chlorophyll, and "singing with the sea," to name a few. The painting one, called "Being Green: Intuitive Painting with Chlorophyll," is described on their website alongside pictures of millennials sitting outside with messy abstract pictures. One photo caption reads, "Students sharing memories of the color green from their childhood."

We spent the first thirty minutes of the ninety-minute journaling class in the parking lot introducing ourselves and describing the last time we saw a wave. I thought back to that photo caption and held in a loud sigh.

I wanted to be in the waves, not hear someone talk about the sunlight hitting the crest of a wave just right three months ago. At the very least I wanted to be standing on the beach, not in the parking lot.

I looked over at Frances and felt grateful she'd been willing to join me on this adventure, even if it should have been clear from the class description what I was getting us into. Standing in the parking lot, it took all my strength to look composed and interested and not shout, *How about we go play in the ocean now instead of talking about it?*

When we finally got to the beach, we got a brief overview of how to nature journal and then spread out to quietly draw for a while. I parked myself by some medium boulders and tried to draw some seagulls swooping around an outcropping of rocks slightly offshore. I scribbled some lines down and distractedly started thinking about what the seagulls were trying to eat. I put some watercolor paint on the page and called it good enough. A solid twenty minutes had passed. I had a shitty painting and was bored.

I wandered from my spot to go find Frances. She, too, was now staring at the ocean. Since we had both doodled something down on the page, we went walking on the beach, "looking for more things to draw." Really we were poking around, investigating and exploring to find crabs and interest-ing-looking shells. A deep noticing, sure, but absolutely not following instructions anymore.

Others (Frances included) were amazing artists. We ended the class with everyone coming back together to show one another our drawings and talk more about being creative in nature. Then we were all given a few drops of an essential oil of some "sacred" plant to rub in our hands and breathe in deeply and think about our connection to nature and creativity.

I had high hopes this tidal pool nature journaling would be a delightful mix of creative practice and being in nature. It has that potential. But this wasn't it. I needed to think about why I disliked it so much.

Chapter 8

Liminality

I really wanted to enjoy nature journaling—I'd love to have notebooks where I wax poetically about grains of sand or the tilt of the sunlight, my words accompanied by deep, colorful drawings in my own unique style. But honestly, the whole thing was a little boring.

One of the instructors showed us her current working notebook. It was gorgeous, filled with snippets of her trips to gardens, to beaches, to different countries. She'd write a few sentences about where she was and who she was with and then pick one aspect to highlight, which she'd then draw with dark lines and colorful watercolor. It seemed like a perfect little journal of a life well-lived, of a practice that both got you deep in the moment and preserved that moment for later. Of recording your life through poetry but with colors.

Then she explained how she went about creating the images. These weren't rough sketches done in the moment. She'd taken photos and made lots of notes and rough sketches—and then later, at home, had drawn and redrawn and watercolored the accompanying images. Her notebook wasn't a snapshot of a time on the beach, but rather a multiday process to create something that looked like a snapshot.

Her notebooks were spectacular. For her, this constituted a deep creative practice she enjoyed and wanted to share with others. Nature journaling seemed to put her in the moment a few different times—both at the beach and later at home—and resulted in something tangible. Why didn't it work for me? Wasn't this exactly what I was looking for?

As I looked at her paintings, part of my brain whispered: But so what? What are you going to *do* with that notebook? Were you actually in the moment when you captured the notes you then needed to revisit? Or when you were at the beautiful spot, were you thinking about how you were going to portray that spontaneous moment later?

It felt like that thing that can happen when things are going super great and your brain whispers *How do I keep this going? How do I get more of this?* And then, bam, you're pulled out of the flow of the moment. Even worse, it felt slightly like an extremely curated analog version of Instagram. Capturing the moment but entirely thought out.

Then the obvious hit me: Her creative practice was art, not craft. She was using the process to express something about those moments in nature. She was an artist.

I'm not an artist. I wanted to craft. The difference between art and craft is muddy. Art is all about expression. It's pure creation. Craft is usefulness.

I wasn't after expressing a feeling. I didn't want to end up with a painting, a photograph, or a song. I wanted something I could use. I wanted to be working toward an end result, an explicit outcome. And when the thing was finished, I wanted to keep using it. I didn't want it all to end with the outcome.

You can use the same tools for both art and craft. It's your intent that creates the distinction. A chair created as art might ask you to question what it means to sit or how one lounges. A chair as craft will try to facilitate that lounge. Both might be beautiful, hand-sawn maple but the purpose will be radically different.

One day I might want to dabble in art. The idea of bringing a notebook and watercolors on some adventure still sounds extremely romantic to me—who doesn't occasionally dream of being Alexander von Humboldt hiking mountains and sketching them? Or, in my case, two more-modern practitioners: Maria Coryell-Martin, the founder of Art Toolkit, who makes tiny watercolor pans and other art supplies to bring on her Arctic glacier expeditions, or the artist Claire Giordano, who backpacks through national parks making watercolors.

But there was a slight flaw in that daydream: It turns out I didn't actually want to do the art itself. Even in the jungle, I now realized, when I felt the itch to do something creative in the heat, it never occurred to me to draw.

Meanwhile I just felt tired and like my to-do list was growing. I couldn't believe I was still in my first trimester, still in the time before I was ready to tell anyone I was pregnant.

After I got home from the first seaweed class with Sophie, I set about figuring out how to dry the seaweed. Our backyard wasn't ideal for drying anything. Berkeley is damp—the clouds roll off the ocean and bump into the Berkeley Hills, creating a thick fog. All of the wooden houses appear to be in some sort of decay. The aging hippies (in their multimillion-dollar homes) don't seem to mind some wood rot and yards scattered with landfill-like "treasures." It seems to be the Berkeley aesthetic, just like bringing your own reusable coffee cup and grocery bags.

In a wonderful way, our rental house blossomed with life. Vines aggressively grew on all the exterior walls, and sometimes into the house itself. The floorboards had rotted through in a few places, revealing the ground beneath. The wooden window frames often seemed like they might just disintegrate when you opened the window. Spiders made webs in most corners. Squirrels had nests in walls. Birds perched just outside and sang lovely songs. The backyard had an overabundance of plants that grew like crazy, no matter how much Sam hacked them back to make room for us. (I got out of all plant-hacking activities. Gardening is one of those weird no-go, high-risk pregnancy activities.)

Every once in a while, hacking back the plants revealed weird trash—keys, cans, pens. I don't know if they were thrown in there by a passersby or "treasures" left by previous tenants. There was plenty of stuff our landlord wouldn't let us throw out: dried out-paint cans, a purple futon, bags of rags, busted chairs, broken birdhouses.

Draping seaweed around the backyard fit the house's modus operandi. I hung it from the clothesline. I put it on baking sheets on the (slowly rotting) picnic table. It took a surprisingly long time given how little seaweed I had actually collected on that first trip—probably at least an hour. Then, after two hours of direct sunlight, the fog rolled in and I needed to go collect it all so it wouldn't rehydrate.

I did this dance for three days. Sunlight: drape it everywhere. Fog: quick, go grab it all. Finally, it had all dried. It felt like I had five pieces of seaweed. Everything had shriveled up into the tiniest pieces. A few of the tiniest got stuck to the baking sheets and when I tried to scrape them off, flaked onto the ground in even smaller bits, disappearing into the dirt and plants.

I wanted to be rejuvenated by the creative endeavor, not drained by it. Diving with the ama—that's rejuvenating. So was tide pooling. But manically running around my backyard moving tiny bits of seaweed around was exhausting.

I took my few dried pieces, stuck them into plastic ziplock bags, and wrote the date and name of the seaweed in permanent marker. Then I looked at the bags. Heidi had given us a recipe for bladderwrack pickles, so I set about making some of that. I emptied my bag of bladderwrack into a mason jar and added some vinegar, salt, and garlic. I screwed on the lid and stuck the concoction in the fridge to pickle, feeling very Bay Area lady of nature. Look at me, I've just gathered something with other women at a specific beach, at a specific time, and then turned it into a tasty snack.

Except I can't tell you if it tasted good or not. I completely forgot about the pickles until cleaning out the fridge months later. I threw the entire thing out, mason jar and all.

The rest of the cooking seaweed languished in plastic bags, pushed further and further into the depths of the pantry. I tried Heidi's suggestion of using the cat's tongue seaweed as a shower exfoliation. It felt like, well, like rubbing seaweed on myself—slimy and a bit silly. I tried a bath with nori seaweed and felt indifferent to the whole experience, mostly wishing I was swimming in the ocean instead of sitting in the tub.

Because Heidi said that the seaweed could be reused, I left both the exfoliating seaweed and the soaking seaweed pieces on the side of the tub to be used at some future time, when certainly it'd feel more relaxing and creative to be using the seaweed like this. Instead, they slowly dried out and then got stuck to the side of the tub. I eventually threw them out too.

Cooking felt like even more work. I felt nauseous. All of a sudden, I only wanted to spend time on my couch. I certainly wasn't going to be spending time standing up in my kitchen cooking new things, or putting seaweed onto pastas, a frequently suggested use. Finding other recipes that went beyond *just throw some seaweed on what you normally eat!* felt too hard.

Plus, all of a sudden food started to feel dangerous. Food has always been my friend. I love eating. But now suddenly I was getting all these confusing messages about what I could eat or not eat and what to be scared of (short answer: seemingly everything).

What if that food was contaminated with listeria? Or salmonella? Or something else? What-ifs swirled in my brain. Even moving my body seemed scary. What if I tripped and fell? What if I twisted too much in a yoga move? What if the bath was too hot? Or the shower? The world started to feel dangerous, and I started to feel small and precarious.

I cried a lot. Everything made me cry. Happy tears. Sad tears. Just tears. All the time. Sam got rid of a spider on a chair outside so I could sit in the sun. I started crying. Because it was so nice of him. Because I worried about her babies—what was going to happen to them now that Sam had just killed their mother?

Pregnancy is not a polite topic. Nothing about it is tidy. And yet, it's during that first trimester that many women choose to be quiet and hidden about their experiences, at least until they get past the major risks of miscarriage. But this is when some of the biggest, unruliest, earth-shattering changes are happening to a pregnant person's body. You're expected to hold a conversation and not spew vomit or feelings.

I felt adrift. It seemed like everything I read was either a magazine article about some heroic woman running a marathon at eight months pregnant or a memoir about how the expectations of motherhood were crumbling women's creative spirits. It all seemed to be championing either aggressive girl power or raw anger. I didn't see myself in either of these messages.

I wanted to read about people who enjoyed pregnancy and motherhood. Where was the "life is pretty good but also I want more ice cream" messaging? Where was the science to help me do risk assessment on food safety? Why were some sources suggesting I drink ginger tea for my nausea and others were telling me it would most likely kill me and the baby? I felt delicate, raw, confused, and bone tired.

All that time lying on the couch gave me a lot of time to think. Why wasn't I out there? Why wasn't I making anything of use? Why did I seem to be pooh-poohing everything? Everyone in the Bay Area seemed to be making something and imagining a new, better world. That's the lore of the place, right?

As I ruminated on my seaweed debacle, I started to wonder if the landscape had something to do with the creativity here. So much of the land is near a coast. You're never far from a tidal zone. And you're often engulfed in fog. The physicality of the environment reminds you that the only constant is change (tidal zones) and to be radically in the present (fog).

Tidal zones (technically called "intertidal zones") are spaces that are regularly exposed to the air and then submerged under the ocean water as the tide washes in. Some of the animals, like clams and mussels, survive this by hiding inside tightly sealed shells. Anemones and seaweed can live for a bit in the air. Still others—octopuses and eels—accidentally get trapped in the tidal zone, stuck in pools of water where they wait for the rising tide to free them.

I identified with these creatures.

Sometimes I was the clam, curled up and hiding, waiting for the next wave of energy to come. Other times I was the seaweed, able to withstand tides and enjoy myself. But more than anything, I felt like an octopus, accidentally caught in a deep pool as the tide receded, unsure of what to do other than just hold tight.

We wax poetic about the journey being the whole point, not the destination. But sometimes the journey sucks. Sometimes you have grand plans to go be a foraging lady of nature and instead find yourself in a ball on the couch, eating ice cream and having your back rubbed.

Yeah, the miracle of life, amazing what my body can do, *blah blah blah*. I felt like shit. I vomited in my mouth. I took naps and then more naps. I cried at everything. I was simultaneously so hungry and didn't want to eat anything. Every ounce of my energy was going toward building something—and it felt like I had been hit by a tsunami.

The thing is, liminal states aren't usually comfortable.

Liminal means being at both sides of a threshold. In pregnancy, you're both yourself from the before times and yourself as a parent to this little being.

In anthropology, there's a related term—*liminality*. It was coined by Arnold van Gennep in his 1909 French book, *Les Rites de Passage*. He was a Dutch-German ethnographer who, as his book title suggests, studied rites of passage.

We have these at key transitions in our lives—marriage, moving, initiations, graduations, funerals. Think of any Pixar or Star Wars film. There's the before, during, and after. It's the classic three-part hero's journey—departure, initiation, and return. Those film scripts rely on Joseph Campbell's *The Hero with a Thousand Faces*, which in turn relied on van Gennep's framework.

What Campbell called *initiation* van Gennep called *liminality*. He used the term to talk about the purposeful disorientation that occurs in the middle stage of a rite of passage—that awful but wonderful messy middle. That confusion helps you mentally transition from the before times to the post-ritual self. If you didn't feel knocked off your feet, would a rite of passage feel as meaningful? Would the movie be as good?

Van Gennep devoted an entire chapter to pregnancy and childbirth. In a way that screams paternalistic today, he wrote about pregnancy ceremonies around the world—from the Toda people of southern India temporarily somewhat separating a pregnant woman from daily life (I can imagine most pregnant women would agree that to not have to *deal* with the regular bullshit feels pretty good) to the Hopi of Arizona stipulating who would be present at the birth to the Bulgarians sheltering the woman and her fetus from "malevolent powers."

Details are vague in van Gennep's writing, but his sentiment is strong: Pregnancy is a time of deep transition for both a woman and her society. Rites help usher along the passage. As he writes, the rites of pregnancy and childbirth "include a passage over or across something, joint prayers and sacrifices, and so forth. One notes the role of intermediaries. Here, as in other ceremonies, they are intended not only to neutralize an impurity or to attract sorcery to themselves but to serve as actual bridges, chains, or links—in short, to facilitate the changing of condition without violent social disruptions or an abrupt cessation of individual and collective life."

It makes sense that almost every society would have guidelines in place to help usher a woman and her community through this transition. We have OB-GYN appointments and baby showers. We track our baby's size compared to vegetables on apps and hire doulas to give us the wisdom we need to make the journey.

In my life, nothing has touched the magnitude of the biological transformation of pregnancy. I started to wonder if the physical changes might also be a rite of passage in their own way. Only two months in and I already felt like I had embarked on a solo adventure where I had left the shore far behind and was now on an ocean, seasick—and I had no idea who I would be when I came to the other shore. Biology seemed to be squarely putting me into liminality.

My body wasn't the same. My mood wasn't the same. My thoughts weren't the same. I felt unmoored. Lost. Not my previous self. Not my future self.

I felt disoriented. But disorientation, as van Gennep wrote, is actually key to the ritual being meaningful. You are in this discrete moment of being in both thresholds—and therefore neither.

You often need to get knocked off your feet for a ritual to be meaningful. Otherwise, it doesn't really shake things up.

Uncertainty helps. You can't make it to the other shore without it.

That doesn't mean the disorientation feels great. I didn't feel like I was going through some wonderful transitioning ritual. I felt lost and confused.

As I groped around looking for a creative outlet, I realized something else: I found I craved instruction. Sometimes life can feel so open-ended and full of decisions that it's nice to have the boundaries found in following a pattern. It can be nice to only have a certain scope within which I can be creative on a project. You know the sweater will likely turn out to be a sweater.

I like that promise. It can make the creative process feel a lot less overwhelming, both to start and to keep going when you're in the messy middle. So much of life is the messy middle. Loving the process is important and all that—what is life but process? But sometimes it's really nice to have a guarantee (or at least a promise) that what you're doing will turn out decent enough. That there's a restfulness in it. For so much in life we're flying by the seat of our pants. There's a comfort in having a creative practice where we don't have to do that.

I wanted something that felt restorative and also gave me something at the end I wanted and could use—so that when creating inevitably hit that messy middle, I had an easy encouragement to keep going. I wanted that promise, even if it was an illusion.

Sea foraging in the Bay Area helped solidify that I love the ocean and eating seaweed—and most certainly do not need to be harvesting my own food as anything but a tourist endeavor. I didn't need to make it more useful than that. I didn't need to feed this baby wild-harvest seaweed or start my own fishmonger business to play in the creative process of sea foraging. I just needed to get in the water.

I had enough of unknowns in my life at that moment. Pregnancy fulfilled that quota.

As I thought about the women I met in Part I, I realized that they were all go big or go home. Whether they were knitters in Denmark or ama in Japan, they obsessed over one creative practice. Did one thing and did it really well. So well that they had made it their job.

Everyone I met so far was all-in on this one thing. To have creativity within your life, how much of your life has to be given over to a single creative practice? Does it need to be your everything? Could I dabble?

Sure, trying out lots of things helps cultivate a beginner's mindset and emphasizes lifelong learning. But it also meant that, as I looked around my house in Berkeley, I saw a half-finished knitted red sock, a fermenting thing of seaweed in my fridge, and a pile of sewing patterns I had printed but never made into clothing. *Oh my god*, I realized, *I might be a dabbler.*

Being a dabbler is the ultimate creative diss—an unkept New Year's resolution, a short attention span, a lack of willpower. It's how someone describes themself if they're trying to downplay their creative pursuit—*oh, I just dabble in watercolor.*

We wax poetically about beginner's mind. As the Zen master Shunryu Suzuki wrote, "In the beginner's mind there are many possibilities, but in the expert's, there are few." That sounds amazing. That sounds enlightened. That doesn't sound like half-finished projects abandoned in the living room.

The dark flip side of that beginner's mind approach within creativity is the dabbler. For me, dabbling feels like always taking classes and never following through—and that that was a bad thing.

Does dabbling count within creativity? Did it make me less-than as someone pursuing creativity? How do we forgive ourselves for dabbling? Do we need to?

Maybe, as they say, I could befriend my shadow self. I could think about dabbling less as distractibility and more as an expression of all-around creativity and exploration. (I should note that however I interpret it, Sam would still like me to tidy up my creative sprawl with some regularity.)

It was time to face some hard facts about my creative practice. What if I wasn't one of these elite creative types with a monk-like focus on a singular practice? What if I was a perpetual beginner? What if I went to a lot of beginner classes? Worse yet, what if I liked that?

Chapter 9

Teachers

With sea foraging I had started to realize that I wanted a creative practice with more instructions. That realization made me start to think again about sewing clothing. If there was one thing I had experienced that had the most A to B instruction, it was sewing. It even has patterns to follow! After my experience with sashiko in Kyoto, I felt ready to return to sewing actual clothing.

Our clothes are both some of the most intimate and public material objects we can possess. I'm not just talking about lingerie. Anything we wear—from the biggest snowsuits to the skimpiest bikinis—falls into this category. We have an intimate, daily, physical relationship with our clothing, whether we think deeply about it or not.

We drape ourselves in various fabrics for shelter and style. You have opinions about it, even if your opinion is in opposition to the concept of fashion or even the concept of clothing itself. (Nudists, after all, might not wear clothing but are defining their lives around the concept of non-clothing.)

I care how clothing looks on me and even more so how it feels on my body. Clothing that doesn't fit right—tugs oddly, scratches, falls off my narrow shoulders, pinches or rubs—drives me insane. It makes it hard for me to focus on anything else. I feel squirmy in my body. I'm aware of the materiality of the clothing item and not in a good way. But clothing that feels good on my body and suits my fashion style is liberating. Freeing. I relax into myself.

That's why I first started knitting: I wanted a cozy sweater that felt good on my body. I hated the ones I was finding in shops. They were scratchy, with tight necks and sleeves that extended way past my hands. Along the way, I discovered that the process of making the sweater made me love it even more when I wore it.

I found a depth in sweaters—the nuances of texture, wool type, color, cuffs, drape, thickness—I hadn't before seen or understood. It was as if an entirely new portal to interacting with the world opened up once I started knitting. I literally saw texture and all fabrics differently.

I figured, well, if I'm going to succumb to my fate of a dabbler who takes a ton of beginner classes, I might as well learn to sew clothing with a great teacher.

Lucky for me, Berkeley was the perfect place to do that. Los Angeles had been intimidating. The fabric shops are for professionals—those that work in the LA fashion industry or are making costumes for the movies. These shops assume you know what you're doing.

Had I known what I was looking for (or even looking at), I would have had a ton of quality options to choose from. Instead, I panicked. When I first attempted to sew myself a linen dress—that ugly lilac muumuu—I didn't go to the many world-class fabric shops of Los Angeles. I bought linen online from a shop in New York City.

I could have tried harder to teach myself to sew clothing from online tutorials and videos—plenty of women did just that during the pandemic—but it just seemed like a lot of effort. I didn't want any more screen time. I wanted real-world teaching.

In Berkeley, I was finding a different atmosphere. There were great fabric shops, like Stonemountain & Daughter, that sold high-end deadstock designer fabric to home sewists who were making their own clothing and quilts. When I popped by, the other shoppers were like me, wanting to make a dress or a sweatshirt. They even hung out together through things like the Bay Area Sewists Meetup group (with membership over 1,000), where they swapped fabric and chatted about patterns.

It was seeming like Berkeley, for all its crunchiness, had better options for holding my hand.

I just needed a teacher. Instagram helped. There I had an account where I mostly followed women sewing, knitting, and sea foraging. Many of them were doing amazing things. Occasionally, I'd see these pictures of a woman named Eli Dembele (@slowsewed) wearing clothes I absolutely wanted to wear and looked perfectly styled on her. Hell, Eli could even make jeans.

Then one day, Eli posted that she was opening a sewing studio in Berkeley. I freaked out—wait, this badass lady not only lives where I just moved, but she also teaches people how to sew their own clothes?

I had to go meet her. I visited Eli's shop, Studio Sessions, during its opening week. Her studio is on one of Berkeley's main commercial strips, an idyllic little downtown area where, within a two-block radius, you've got a pizza shop, a coffee shop, a candle shop, a bookstore, a movie theater—and now, a sewing studio.

Eli is French and moved to Northern California almost a decade ago with her French husband. When she first arrived, she couldn't find clothes that fit her aesthetic. So she set about figuring out how to make her own. First, she needed to learn how to sew. She did that so well, and with such singular focus, that she now teaches others to sew their own clothing.

They say don't meet your heroes. But, so far, all the women I'd met on this creativity quest had been as badass as I had imagined them to be. The ama, Kazue stitching in Kyoto, the Danish knitwear designers, the sea-foraging instructors of the Bay Area, and now, Eli here in Berkeley. I kept being pleasantly surprised: They were astonishingly talented and fun to be around.

I immediately signed up for a workshop, a two-day class focused on making a cotton twill French chore jacket. I chose maroon as my color. I, along with three other women, spent two days at Eli's studio sewing and laughing.

Eli was three steps ahead of us, always. We didn't need to follow written pattern instructions (although she gave us some to take home)—Eli had memorized each step. She would look over at someone pausing and tell them their next step in the pattern instructions. Somehow she was paying attention to all of us sewing at once.

You'd hear someone sewing at a machine say, *Oh no . . . Eli?* And she'd be over there in a split second, helping them unjam a machine, redo a seam line, or attach a button. Or, in my case, figure out how I managed to sew a sleeve to the neck hole . . . twice in a row.

The entire time she cheered us on, letting us know we could do it and were doing great. She kindly laughed when she saw I had sewn the sleeve to the neck and then helped me lay out the pieces on her gigantic cutting table so I wouldn't do it a third time.

Good teachers push you but make you feel capable. They help you stretch and see new possibilities.

I walked away from the weekend with new friends and a wearable, cute jacket. It had utility—you need jackets and lots of them in the Bay Area. As my pregnancy progressed, the pockets proved invaluable as I carried around a boatload of snacks. And it didn't look like anything an old granny would wear. It didn't look homemade at all. It looked tailored to me—but not done by me.

Research is what I do best. I love diving deeply into a topic I know nothing about and asking lots of questions—of books and humans. If, as I was realizing, pregnancy was another creative practice, well then I had better start using my research abilities. Surely (obviously), I wasn't the first woman to have ever been pregnant before.

Near the beginning of my second trimester, I bought all the books. Most were dumb and hyperbolic. Some weren't. In particular, Emily Oster's *Expecting Better* held my hand in all the ways I wanted guidance. Here was another woman who likes numbers, facts, and reading research papers. I wasn't the only woman who so desperately wanted data and science, not fear mongering.

When Oster, a professor of economics at Brown University, first got pregnant almost a decade ago, she was taken aback by the arbitrariness of the supposed rules. She wanted to know: Where's the data behind these alleged rules and scary things so often told to pregnant women? No one could give her solid answers, so she started reading the studies for herself—and then later for her friends.

The data on what pregnant women should or should not do is often imperfect, subjective, and individual. Oster isn't telling people to *do this, not that.* Instead, she's helping women contextualize subjective risk and make informed decisions for themselves. She reminds women: How do you contextualize risk and tradeoffs? Life is only full of risks. What are worth taking and what aren't? Imperfect data can still be helpful. It can empower women.

When I did start to panic about something, instead of spiraling, I'd get Sam to help. *Tell me the data. Find the numbers. Tell me risk context.* Was the cheese I so much wanted to eat fine? What about coffee? I just wanted a damn cup of coffee.

For the most part, the answer was: Just let your body do its thing and kinda get out of the way. Sleep a lot. Drink lots of fluids. Eat what you feel like (and sign up for FDA and CDC listeria outbreak text alerts). Relinquish control.

Oster's approach calmed my panic. But I still felt unsteady physically. As my body started to grow and my internal organs, spine, and pelvis started to shift around to create space for this growing baby, my body felt unfamiliar and achy. My sacrum hurt. I moved about awkwardly—I felt like a pile of blocks unevenly balanced. My center of gravity had shifted, but my body and brain hadn't figured out to where.

I needed in-person pregnancy mentors, not just books. In nearby Albany, I found Debbie Lai, a body movement specialist with a background in Pilates and yoga and a focus on pregnant and postpartum women.

Debbie's background comes from an expert-expert level of knowledge. She didn't just go to some retreat once and start calling herself wise about bodies. In fact, it's the opposite. She's got a deep level of knowledge that comes from years of practice and learning from some of the best teachers. Debbie is almost annoyingly humble and full of knowledge—that adage of the wiser you get, the more you understand how little you know.

Debbie taught me how to stand. Yes, literally stand. I had been throwing my hips forward, tucking my pelvis and keeping my feet wide apart in an attempt to steady myself against the growing belly. Most pregnant women do this— think of the arching spine, hands on the lower back, wide-legged waddle you see in so many pregnant bodies.

But, untucking your pelvis, bringing your diaphragm and lower ribs out of a splayed, arching position, and keeping your feet only hip-distance apart stacks the bricks of your pregnant body in a much more comfortable way.

All of a sudden, existence became a lot easier. Debbie and I went about helping me safely move my body and start working out again. We did the gentlest of Pilates, getting all those tiny stabilizing muscles firing. I went from hurting all over to being able to stand for long chunks of time.

There's something to be said about finding physical stability that then helps you find it mentally. I had spent so much of my first trimester feeling unmoored.

Debbie understood how individual bodies are and how much that individuality permeates pregnancy. That individuality was one of the hardest parts of pregnancy for me. So much of the guidance was a vague "listen to your body."

It felt like the repercussion of a creativity explosion—you've decided to channel Georgia O'Keeffe and have all the paints and inspiration. Now your canvases are covered in a muddy acrylic mix, not beautiful Southwest vistas and flowers. The mess part of a creative mess.

Working out with Debbie made me feel good but even more importantly she helped me think about my body in space—of how my brain could support my body as it went about its own creative practice of being pregnant. So much of our lives—and how I was approaching these other creative practices, like sewing—is brain-first. I like moving my body, but I'm often in my head. I like it there.

I can also overthink things. In pregnancy, that didn't help. Trusting my body to do its own creative practice, of which my brain was along for the ride and not the driver, was the only way to sanely get through pregnancy.

I couldn't think my way into growing the baby's limbs and muscles. I could think about how I was standing: Was my pelvis tucked? How wide apart were my legs? Using my brain to periodically redirect my posture let me stand without being in pain, let my brain feel like it was part of the pregnancy creative practice in a way that wasn't just ruminating anxiety loops.

It let me think about other things, like sewing coats and dresses. I could now comfortably stand long enough to actually sew them—and do all the (mostly standing) steps before you sit down to actually sew.

This whole working one-on-one with a teacher thing was really working for me. It made me want to work more with Eli on sewing things for my individual body. What I needed most of all, right then, was pregnancy clothing. Simply unbuttoning the top button of my pants wasn't working anymore.

Soon after that French chore jacket workshop, I emailed Eli asking if she'd be willing to teach me more sewing. I wanted to learn it all—techniques, fit, different materials, any and all of it. I wanted to be picky about colors and what fabrics I put against my sensitive skin. I wanted cute buttons on things that made me look elegant—but that I could also throw into a washing machine.

I wanted someone to teach me how to do it. If I was going to be a dabbling lady who takes lots of beginner classes, I wanted great teachers along the way. I wanted to dabble, sure, but I wanted to dabble well.

Eli met my request with an offer: She was designing a capsule wardrobe course and wanted me to guinea pig it for her. We'd go through the entire course together and I'd offer feedback.

I should pause here and explain: Eli, being French, understands the concept of a capsule wardrobe much differently than most Americans do. We think capsule wardrobe and immediately see twenty pieces of bland clothing that can be "mixed and matched."

Eli means it in the French way: a distinct set of clothes for an occasion, like a vacation or springtime—or, say, maternity or postpartum.

Her focus with the capsule wardrobe program was helping students define their style and expand their skills. It would be ambitious, with a lot of individualized work on her end. She could have simplified it down to five pieces that all students could make and somewhat tailor to themselves. I asked her why she didn't do that—it would have been a lot easier (and more in line with what I had historically thought of as a capsule wardrobe). *That's boring, Sarah* was the smiling reply from Eli. She doesn't want conformity—she wants to help students express themselves.

Me being me, I came to Eli with probably like six years' worth of sewing project ideas. Eli helped me focus. She made me think about what I owned and why. What I wanted to own. What felt good on me. What I liked. What inspired me. For inspiration, she pushed me to think widely. She told me she often got ideas on hikes—she'd see two colors paired together on a bird and realize that combination would look great in an outfit.

As I entered my second trimester, I was starting to get a belly and realizing just how few items in my closet would soon fit me for the many months ahead. I wanted pieces I could wear in Berkeley's fall and winter as a pregnant lady. I wanted the items to be able to fit my expanding body. I wanted to use these pieces, not just as lovely things in my closet, but as learning opportunities.

We'd meet a few times a week at Eli's studio—usually for a couple of hours at a time. Then, at my house, I'd work on the projects until the next time we met.

When I thought about sewing my own clothing, I imagined sitting at a sewing machine for hours at a time. I had forgotten that almost 80 percent of the sewing process isn't sewing. As I was figuring out, sewing any piece of clothing is almost always a multi-hour, if not a multiday, process.

First you need to research and pick out the pattern. Then research and buy your fabric. Wash/dry and iron your fabric (wash/dry it how you intend to later wash/dry it).

Measure yourself in the necessary areas per the pattern requirements. Figure out what size of the pattern you are. Decide whether to print out just that size (if it's a fancy PDF) or print out the whole thing. Then decide: Am I getting a professional to print this on an A0 giant single sheet of paper (ideal but takes a few days) or am I using my home printer right this second to print out a million pieces of regular printer paper and tape them all together?

Next use a highlighter to mark the lines on the printed paper pattern that are for your size—the cutting lines (which are different than the seam/sewing lines) and the different marks (notches for matching together pattern pieces, button placements, pocket placements, etc.).

Now put tracing paper over that and trace all those lines and marks. Make sure you label all the pattern pieces with their names (Left Arm, Front Pocket, Piece A, etc.). Cut out the tracing pattern pieces. Or, skip the tracing paper and cut it direct out on the paper pattern (which is fine but means if you end up ever wanting to make the pattern in a different size, you have to reprint it).

Pin the paper pattern pieces on your already washed, dried, and ironed fabric. This might not even be your final fabric. It's technically a smart idea to always do a trial run of the entire process with some cheap fabric, often called muslin, so that if you want to make size adjustments or you mess things up on the first run, you're doing it on cheap fabric, not your fancy stuff. A smart idea that can basically double the amount of time it takes to make something.

Cut out the fabric using the paper pattern pieces as templates. Make sure you're cutting on the cutting lines, which will be a certain amount away (called a seam allowance) from where you'll eventually sew. Make sure you are transferring all important marks—notches, pocket placements, etc.—onto the fabric itself with a washable or heat eraser pen (a Pilot Frixion one works well) and/or using thread to make tailor's knots.

It is only now that you can begin sewing. Look at step 1 of your instructions and start from there. Ideally, as Eli kept reminding me, you already read those instructions when you first started this whole process. I *mostly* did actually read the instructions ahead of time and definitely always at least skimmed them.

I loved learning with Eli. She's this amazing teacher who'd casually offer perspective-altering statements. One time, she looked over at me fighting the sewing machine, trying to yank the fabric in a different direction under the pounding needle. *Sarah*, she said, *sewing is like driving. You look where you're going, not where you are. When you drive, you look ahead to see where the potholes are. You don't swerve once you're already on top of them.*

My five-piece plan was to make a coat, a dress, a long-sleeve shirt, and a jumpsuit, and alter some thrift shop jeans into maternity pants. That got derailed by my pregnancy pretty quickly. I ended up with two coats, a jacket, and two dresses. I wanted warmth, and I wanted flowy.

I made two long, boiled wool coats (one black, one purple and gray), a hip-length green teddy fleece chore jacket, a viscose linen dress with front buttons, and a wrap dress in a rusty red cotton. I found these patterns, with Eli's help, the same way I found my knitting patterns: indie female designers marketing their patterns through hip Instagram accounts.

Everything had pockets—deep pockets (for an easily accessible trail mix bag). Everything was soft. I felt cuddled by all the items. They all fit my narrow shoulders. No sleeve length was too long. All the items looked elegant with hidden playful touches, like speckled buttons, floral interiors, cheeky tags. I suddenly had a lot of things in my wardrobe that felt me.

Usually when an item feels *me* in my closet, it's because I've worn it so much. Like my threadbare merino T-shirts I've had for fifteen years. They're so worn they're see-through. They feel me not because they necessarily express my style but because they've spent miles and hours on my body. They're me by association. These new pieces felt like me by choice.

Before sewing with Eli, I hadn't thought about that aspect of use. That yeah, I wanted utility—but now I also had expression within that utility. It turns out it did feel good to have some of that artistic expression. What I was expressing, it turns out, wasn't a feeling or thought, but me.

That's great to think about—that you're expressing yourself through a creative practice. But also, it gets annoyingly frustrating. It's amazing to think about how you're making a jacket that feels oh so you—less so when it isn't turning out how you hoped it would look.

If you mess up any of the above steps before you sit down at a sewing machine, you make your life a lot harder.

For example, I would sometimes mis-cut things. Twice I cut pieces backward. Backward because not only is there usually a front and back to the fabric, but there's often left and right pattern pieces, which look similar but are actually mirror images of each other. (I had second trimester energy boosts, but I also very much had pregnancy brain.)

There was no fixing these two mis-cuts. For one of them, I luckily had enough fabric to just recut the entire piece again. The other time I did it—on the black boiled wool coat's lining sleeves—I didn't have enough extra fabric to cut another piece, and the shop was completely sold out.

I really liked the lining fabric I had originally picked out—it was a silky rayon, a navy background with flower bouquets. I wanted a sleek look on the outside but a pop of colorful beauty on the inside. I didn't want a new inside to the coat. I wanted to not have had made a dumb mistake.

Eli took my sadness seriously. She knew it wasn't just fabric. But she also knew: I was only missing fabric for the inside of the sleeves. It didn't need to match. I could still have my flower bouquets: No one sees the inside of coat sleeves— that fabric could be different.

Eli has this great ability to home in on what matters and let the other parts be squishy. When I casually said, *Jeans are impossible. No way I'll ever be able to make those*, Eli got a serious look on her face and said, *What? No. That's wrong. They just take time because there's a lot of details that matter.*

When I'm sewing, I get an energized buzzing—like I'm engaged with life. It's a nice mix of productive and taking time purely for myself.

All of a sudden, the parts I thought you had to rush through to get to the "real" sewing had become just part of the whole process. There's a pretty obvious metaphor here about approaching life this way. As they say, the interruptions are life, and the journey is the way. The whole point of sewing is the process—otherwise go buy a finished thing from someone else. It's the *-ing* part, not the sewn part, that you're actually after in this creative practice. That's obviously true of all creative practices but somehow seems so starkly true of sewing when you think about why make your own shirt when you could just go buy one.

A good teacher helps you play in that process part. Helps you see a goal, go after it—and keep going when you've run into a wall. Someone like Eli helps you realize that you haven't ruined it all, it's fixable. And, in retrospect, like my black coat's secret mismatched sleeve linings, that visible mistake is a nice reminder when I put the coat on of *Hey, you made this thing— yes you!* I could dream big because I knew Eli had my back.

Chapter 10

Community

If I didn't have to go it alone for pregnancy or even sewing, I started to wonder about all sorts of delineations. Where was the line between making something and not? Clearly I was making this baby. Though, uh, I didn't do that alone.

Could I say I made the clothing with guidance? That I made it myself? There's no way I would have come away with a wearable (much less a fashionable) coat had I tried to create it on my own. But even with Eli's help, it wasn't just the two of us. We didn't make the materials—of the coat or the tools.

You can get a bit dizzily exponential here—the designer of the pattern, the shearer of the sheep, the dyer of the fabric.

I wasn't shearing sheep to make the boiled wool exterior of my black boiled wool coat. I hadn't designed my purple one (Ella, a woman living in San Francisco with the Instagram handle @handmademillennial, had done that). I certainly hadn't spun the thread or manufactured my sewing machine. But at the end of creating both my coats, I felt like I had made them.

What amount of a project do you have to do by yourself? Can you do just the fun parts—and cut out the annoying parts? Is that skipping the "journey" only for the destination—or just making the journey a bit more pleasant?

Does sewing from a kit count as creativity? Painting by numbers? You're certainly following instructions.

Few people would count painting by numbers as creative, but you are making something. You're in the flow of painting. You're probably in a similar state of mind induced by making something. How is following a sewing pattern any different?

Even Eli's French chore jacket workshop had taken out a lot of the painful bits—the tedious pattern printing, cutting, serging, even the fabric sourcing and finding the right buttons. All we had to do was assemble, which was more than enough for me as a beginner sewist. Afterward, I proudly told every person I could that I had made my jacket as I wore it around Berkeley.

Putting aside that I wasn't going to grow my own cotton plants or tend some sheep, is creativity something you have to earn by making everything from scratch?

It's a strawman argument anyway, huh? We are never in isolation. Never fully detached from others and their contributions to the world. You're never entirely making anything alone. That doesn't mean you're not making. Sewing my capsule wardrobe items, I was still making something—both creating and personalizing.

I'd sew with Eli and then go home and sew some more. If I got stuck, I'd start sewing other things. I made zippered pouches for tiny things, a hot pink silk pajama top, and a blue fleece bathrobe. In theory, I liked Eli's approach of a capsule wardrobe. That one should create a plan and see one project to completion before moving on to the next one. But I didn't actually follow that when I was sewing at home.

Making my own clothes felt deeply luxurious. In a good way. Following instructions of a sewing pattern didn't feel lobotomizing. Instead, it felt like meditation instructions. Someone is showing you the path, sure. That doesn't mean you don't then have to go walk it yourself.

As I started to sew more with Eli, I realized just how big the whole community of other sewists making their own clothing is. Some of that community was digital, through a home sewing projects app called Threadloop. Eli told me about it. I had come into her studio carrying my red notebook stuffed with pieces of scrap paper—helpful in scrawling notes, but somewhat impossible to find information when I needed it later. I asked her how she organizes her notes on her many sewing projects—her beautiful handwriting (the French write in cursive because it's faster) in her notebook was the answer. Eli suggested I look into Threadloop, which was still in beta testing.

I did—and loved it. Two Norwegians design it: Guro Lindahl Flåten, a software designer and home sewist, and Endre Johnsen, Guro's partner and also a software designer. Threadloop lets you record all your patterns, fabrics, thread spools, buttons, etc.—as well as your notes and photos for each project.

Then there's the community aspect: You can search and contribute to a database of patterns. Threadloop then lets you share your projects and notes, leave public reviews on patterns (were the instructions hard to understand, but the result is worth it?), and create curated lists (e.g., best linen tees for summer). It's an asynchronous conversation with others also sewing at home—about home sewing by home sewists.

I had known the internet could provide community— or a semblance of one. I had seen all of these home sewists tagging one another on Instagram. But I've never felt very comfortable on social media—I get too much in my head about its performative and permanent nature to casually make connections there. Others certainly had. Eli's shop grew, in part, out of her Instagram account's popularity.

Threadloop felt a bit more in the right direction. For one, it's more secluded. You're only there for sewing. And it's not trying to provide deep community.

It is a stilted conversation. It's shallow. I think of that as light-touch community. You're only thinking of one thing. You're not sharing much of yourself. But still, shallow community is important. Threadloop feels like the sewing equivalent of knowing your barista's name or saying hi to the mail carrier.

For a deeper community, Eli came to my aid once again. Every month, there's a two-hour "Scrap Night" at the studio. As the website description says, "Bring friends or make friends here."

At Scrap Night, you can bring any hand-sewing project you want to work on. Women, mostly in their thirties and forties, work on making the ruffles on a dress, hemming a shirt, patching a pant leg, and so on. Mostly, they make quilts. Hexi quilts to be specific. It's an English paper piecing quilting technique where you sew together little two-inch hexagons in flowerlike arrangements until you slowly have a big blanket. It's always been a staple of American quilting and is having a resurgence among millennial sewists.

The technique lets you use up any small scraps you might have and pick up and put down the sewing whenever you feel like it. If you don't already have your own scraps but want to join in the fun, you can even buy a cute little kit from Eli's shop with all the materials and tools to get started.

Hand sewing shines with these types of projects. You could make a hexi quilt on a machine, but it wouldn't be the same. Some of the best parts are the repetitive hand motions and the ability to do something (parallel play) while others do the same. It's easier to chat while hand sewing than machine sewing.

And it's much easier to bring your sewing project with you. The women at Scrap Night wouldn't just sew their hexi quilts at the once-a-month meet-up; they brought their projects everywhere. On road trips, to the beach, to watching their kids' soccer practices. Anywhere I'd have brought my knitting, they bring their sewing.

Hand sewing seems to infuse more love into a garment. It is slower. More thoughtful. Quieter. More like knitting. It feels much more for the delight in the process, whereas machine sewing is very much about the end result.

The imperfections of hand sewing show a human hand. When you wrap yourself in a quilt, that humanness is part of what you're after. Using material like scraps and old fabric makes it feel extra loved—already worn in, like an old flannel that hugs you just right. Because isn't what you want from a handmade quilt, right? A big hug.

As with sashiko, sewing the hexi pieces was relaxing and meditative. I liked hand sewing and chatting—all the women I met at these Scrap Nights were delightful and interesting. Having sewing be the main focus let our conversations range wildly into unexpected destinations. I can't imagine that our conversations would have been as deep and unguarded had we each not had a project in our lap.

But the sewing outcome—the hexi quilts—just aren't my thing. So, I sewed at Scrap Nights for the community—but not the quilt.

I learned a surprising term at one of these Scrap Nights—selfish sewing. We were chatting about cute kid patterns. One of the women was asked if she also sewed for her family members. She laughed and said, *Oh no. I'm a selfish sewist. I only make things for myself.*

I was taken aback by this. Why did that make her selfish? Searching online at home, I learned that selfish sewing was a pretty common term. Something a lot of women who sew wrestle with. It seemed to be a dichotomy—are you selfish or do you mostly sew things for others?

It didn't occur to me that one might delineate so rigidly. In thinking about it, I squarely fit into the camp of selfish sewists. I only really want to make things for myself. I have no interest in making Sam a boiled wool coat, though I'd like to make myself a few more. If Sam wants a handmade one, he's welcome to learn how to make it himself.

Why would I feel guilty about spending my creative time making things for myself? Clearly this is something a lot of these women struggled with. It confused me.

I didn't understand how my approach to sewing is selfish. I mean, I'd argue that the reverse is true: Only allowing yourself to be creative if it is making things for others seems pretty shitty to me. If you don't do things for yourself, it's easy to get into a trap of resenting the others around you.

There's a reason that airlines tell you to put on your own oxygen mask first. You can't help others if you can't breathe. There's also a reason they have to repeat those instructions every damn flight. It's all too easy to forget that you need to care for yourself before you're of any use to anyone else.

Why would creativity be any different?

When I find myself getting a bit too enthusiastic about my own perspective and not understanding why someone else might do something differently, I ask my sister her opinion.

Fiona sees the whole idea of selfish sewing as a false dichotomy. She makes herself dresses, pants, ceramic butter holders, hydrating facial oils, wool sweaters . . . everything. She doesn't define that as selfish—she wants some nice rose hip body oil and so she crafts it. She unabashedly nurtures her own creativity. And yet, she also loves making things for others—her partner, Cyrus, has a growing collection of Fiona sweaters.

I asked her why she makes things for other people—why not spend that time on yourself? After giving me her classic *"Oh Sarah . . ."* sigh when I'm overthinking something she thinks normal people just understand, she explained: Making things for others is one of her ways to express her love for the recipient. It doesn't detract from her ability to also craft for herself.

It's clear to see that love when you look at the growing pile of things Fiona has made for my baby. A hand-sewn quilt depicting an abstract outdoorsy scene of sun and mountains made from naturally dyed linen and cotton that Fiona bought in various places on her world travels. Tiny socks from leftover yarn of a sweater Fiona just finished for herself. A small cream sweater with blue and green stripes. The love Fiona feels is explicitly tangible and very soft.

I know Fiona got that approach from our parents. When I was in graduate school at Yale, I once needed a better desk—the one that came with my apartment wiggled with each keyboard stroke and was just absolutely the wrong size. My dad drove up three hours with his woodworking tools, and we went to Home Depot for supplies. In my apartment's backyard (in the snow, nonetheless), he sawed and drilled and sanded—as I stood by and "helped" (I've never been very useful at being a woodworking assistant). A few hours later, I had a customized desk that fit into the corner of my room perfectly and was the right height so that my shoulders didn't hurt from hours of hunching over a laptop.

That was only from pure love and support of what I was trying to do at grad school. As Fiona was insisting now, just because my dad made me something didn't mean he doesn't make a lot of other woodworking projects for himself—there's a reason the smell of freshly cut wood makes me think of home.

Plus, as Fiona continued to explain, sometimes it's more fun to make things for others who will be amazed at what you made rather than see all the mistakes. Perfectionism can be a sticky wicket in all creative acts.

As I thought about selfish sewing and the all-too-easy ways to curtail our fun within creativity, I started to see the obvious parallels with pregnancy and motherhood.

Selfish sewing isn't actually selfish—it's attending to your needs. You're making a baby's life, but you're also making your own.

In these liminal times of pregnancy, so much was changing. I needed a new wardrobe, and sewing things for myself and my pregnant body was more interesting than crafting for a yet-to-be-born baby or some other human.

Motherhood and pregnancy so often get cast as the ultimate martyrdom experience. Here I was, very much uncomfortable in my body, which was putting seemingly all its energy toward building a baby. It seemed all too easy of a next step to put all my energy toward the kid in motherhood, too.

And yet, giving up your creative pursuits because you have kids—or only doing them for the kids—seems like the equivalent of knitting someone an ugly, itchy sweater and forcing them to wear it because you spent hours making it. The kid doesn't want that. Those sweaters make your skin crawl.

I didn't want that. I thought about how I'd keep up creative practices as I became a mother. I didn't quite have a plan or really much thought about it other than *don't get into the mindset that doing what brings you joy is selfish.*

Luckily, the women at Scrap Night seemed to be reading my thoughts. On one of the nights, as we all sewed our hexi quilts, a woman I had just met looked at my large belly and gently asked: *Can I give you some unsolicited advice?* It's hard to say no in that situation, so I said yes.

She said: *Don't stop doing the things that make you you. Don't wait until they're older to get back into creative things. Life always gets in the way. Set up your life—and your family's expectations—now. It's harder to do it later on. My youngest is now eleven, and I'm only now getting my creative practice back. I told myself I'd get back to it but then life got in the way. You think it'll only be for a little bit, but then you turn around and it's been a decade.*

Don't let false practicality get in the way of being yourself. As a runner, I thought about adventure and athlete mothers I admired: Chelsey Magness (mountain biker), Serena Williams (tennis), Kimi Werner (free diving), Allyson Felix (sprinter), Belinda Baggs (surfing), and so many more. These women keep doing their badass training and competing at the most elite levels. They're doing it not despite having children but because they have them. Doing what they love makes them fuller people and better mothers.

Plus, a fact I love to hold on to as a runner: If female runners take care of themselves enough in the postpartum time, studies show that most go on to run faster races after they become mothers.

I'm pretty sure it's true of other sports as well. As Chelsey Magness, the extremely accomplished mountain bike racer, wrote in her essay "How Motherhood Made Me a More Successful Pro Athlete" on the website GearJunkie, "Motherhood has been an amazing journey full of ups and downs. Never in a million years could I have told you that I would be a better athlete after having kids. But it is the truth." She continues, "And not only do I think I am a better athlete, but I am also a better partner, friend, daughter, sister, and human since becoming a mother as well. The gifts from all of my boys are endless, and I am eternally grateful and humble."

Yes, being pregnant means you're making a life. But you're also making your own life. It presented daunting and intriguing questions: How would I keep going after my own creative pursuits? How was I going to let motherhood expand my existence?

Chapter 11

Flow States

Before I realized how much I really enjoyed making stuff for myself, I had plans to make things for this baby. I bought patterns for nightgowns, onesies, jumpers, and pants. But each time I had a bit of time to start a new project, I kept choosing myself. Funnily enough, I started to choose knitting. Not the act of knitting itself, but sewing things for knitting.

I realized I could make knitting accessories. Like bags to hold all my different knitting projects, tools, and extra yarn. I made zipper pouches, tote bags, and a set of drawstring bags in three different sizes, made out of Japanese canvas with yellow and white daisies on a light blue background and a lilac cord for the drawstrings. I put my red sock in one.

Compared to the challenging sewing projects Eli and I were tackling together in my capsule wardrobe course, these small side projects were easy. They were what I had imagined all sewing would be: pick a pattern on a whim, grab some pretty fabric at the shop, cut it, sew up a new thing, and go use it.

It felt like I'd been let in on a magic trick. Before sewing with Eli, piecing together something as simple as a drawstring bag felt incomprehensible, even with instructions. Then, somewhere along the way, I got it. One day, I realized I understood how to put together flat pieces of fabric, how to fold the fabric at the top of the bag so that then I could slip in a string making the simple container into a drawstring bag.

I made a lot of these side projects in the middle of my second trimester when I had an abundance of energy. I figured that high of energy might possibly last forever, despite what everyone else and all the literature told me.

In the third trimester, however, the logistics started getting a lot harder. My belly was growing seemingly exponentially. Reaching things at the sewing table got harder, and Eli started helping me cut out the fabric patterns. She took out more than one seam I'd incorrectly sewn as my brain turned to mush—a time-consuming and laborious act of tiny rips. Only pure generosity could drive one to undo someone else's mis-sewn seams.

Then the fatigue hit hard. All I wanted to do was flop onto my couch. But like with most pregnant women, no position felt comfortable. I wanted to face-plant. Can't do that with a pregnant belly. I wanted to lie on my back. Can't do that because of how your organs reorganize to make space for the belly and then put pressure on an important blood vein (the inferior vena cava) if you lie on your back. The best ergonomic option, lying on my side, was boring. I spent countless hours awake at night in that position and balked at the idea of doing more of it.

In my first and second trimesters, I had had enough energy to pace around, to be in "active seated positions" (aka bouncing on an exercise ball instead of sitting in a chair), or to distract myself from my increasing sacrum pain with a sewing project. Now, I was exhausted standing. I was exhausted lying down.

Healthcare practitioners kept telling me this inability to lie on the couch and really only be in upright positions or moving was a blessing in disguise. It was helping keep my body in the best ergonomical positions for the later stages of third trimester and for delivery—baby head down with his back on my left side. I didn't want a blessing in disguise. I wanted to lounge.

This is where the genius of Debbie, the body movement specialist, once again saved me. I came into her office practically crying about my exhaustion and desire to rest. I figured, like everyone else, she'd tell me the benefits of sitting on an exercise ball instead of a chair. She suggested a different option: a supported squat.

I imagined an intense CrossFit-like exercise and might have suggested to her that she was a crazy person for asking me to do it. She laughed and showed me what she meant. A stack of two yoga blocks with a meditation bolster on top as a cushion. You sit with your heels near the blocks in a squat position and your knees bent, practically hitting your elbows. It's a pretty relaxed active seated position. You're not doing strenuous physical work, and the pressure was off my sacrum. I could relax. I could watch TV. I could sit and zone out. I could knit.

Which was great—because all of a sudden, I wanted to knit, not sew. I wanted the slow, repetitive motions of knitting. It's some movement, some progress but not a lot of physical exertion. I could still feel the guise of productivity.

I guess we like what we like. I could have just kept on going with the hexi quilt at home. That would've given me literally all the same things I was looking for in a creative project in my third trimester.

That's the beauty of creative practices—I probably could have picked any random assortment of crafts and gotten the same underlying tenets of intentionality and flow. The whole genre of men fixing motorcycles fits that definition.

Even more so, hexi quilt creation and knitting are almost the same: slow, repetitive hand movements that build a snuggly thing. But at the end of the day, I want a sweater. Not a blanket. I don't knit blankets.

The Sailor Sweater that I was knitting in Denmark was half-finished, mostly untouched. But as I started to feel that itch for knitting again, I didn't pick up the Sailor Sweater. I bought yarn to start a different sweater, a cardigan. I'd become hyper-focused on the idea that I needed a cardigan for breastfeeding—modest easy access for all those times I was going to be out and about.

I'm really not great at the whole finish-one-project-at-a-time thing. If I'm honest, sometimes it feels a lot easier to be at the shiny new start phase of a project than the messy middle. When I'm stuck at a part of a project—whether in knitting, sewing, writing, life, whatever—it always feels like a better, easier option to go start something new than push through the sluggish middle.

Somehow in this new project, I tell myself, I'll be more productive and skilled. The idea of doing the colorwork knitting on the Sailor Sweater seemed tedious, so I picked up a new project. Did I pick an easier one? No, of course not. I picked one that was so much harder, somehow thinking that I'd have more energy and focus.

We all do this to different degrees. It has taken me a long time to learn that this is part of the creative process—that a new project is always shiny and the messy middle is consistently rough. To keep the spark of creativity alive, sometimes you gotta lean into these unrealistic fantasies. If you knew all the potholes ahead, you might not start out on the journey at all. The trick, of course, is to keep the fantasy slightly obtainable—and find ways to not get demoralized when you inevitably stumble.

The cardigan pattern was by the Danish designer Mette Wendelboe Okkels, the one with the huge Instagram following who is good at math She named it the Agnete Cardigan. It's a sleek-looking, ribbed, button-down cardigan with some structure, with a suggested yarn combination of merino, silk, and mohair Isager yarns. That sleekness comes from the design and combination of the high-quality yarns, but it also is a result of the tiny-sized needles used and some incredibly hard knitting techniques.

PetiteKnit sweater designs are rated on a 1-to-5 scale of difficulty. The highest I'd done before this cardigan was a 3. The Agnete is a 5. I had never attempted almost all of the knitting techniques. Why I thought this was a good time to go for it is somewhat of a mystery. Mostly it was that I wasn't thinking about the practicality of making the cardigan—I was thinking about the end result. I suppose it's necessary that we have these fantasies when starting out on something, be it signing up for a race, starting a painting, or cooking an elaborate meal. But sometimes the result is a belly flop.

The knitting needles used for making the Agnete Cardigan are so small that I had to go buy new needles. All of the local yarn shops didn't sell needles that small. I finally found them for sale on a niche knitting website.

On top of this, I added to the degree of difficulty by choosing a gorgeous navy yarn. Dark-colored yarn can be difficult to knit with, because it's much harder to see the individual knots. A black sweater is only a labor of love and determination.

Somehow, I convinced myself that this was going to be much easier than just finishing the Sailor Sweater. Messy middles can make us do silly things.

When I'm at an intimidating part in a knitting project, I like to take it to a coffee shop. I sit there for an hour or two, listen to the nice music, hear the hiss of the espresso machines, and bribe myself with good caffeine and baked goods.

Once I assembled all the necessary yarn, needles, and instructions, I realized that even step 1 was going to be hard. (Usually, it's not until step 3 that I start getting overwhelmed.) So instead of quitting the cardigan before I even started, I stuffed all the supplies into a tote bag I had sewn myself and headed to CoRo, one of my favorite coffee shops in Berkeley.

It's in this odd part of Berkeley that looks like abandoned warehouses. Some are, but most are chemistry labs that are private or somewhat related to the university. CoRo is nestled among these warehouses because it's also a roaster. It roasts its own coffee and lets other small coffee companies roast there as well. That means it's the best, freshest coffee in Berkeley.

Through giant windows you can watch them roast the beans, and it always smells like burnt caramel from the bean roasting. The vibes are distinctly friendly and chill. There's not much seating, but you can usually always find a seat. It feels like sitting in a nerd-filled library of adults. People are writing papers, discussing physics, sketching their cups of coffee.

Headphones on, I watched YouTube tutorials for the cast-on techniques to begin the cardigan, rewinding them more than twenty times as I tried to copy the tutorial, messed it up, and tried again. Eventually, I started to get it. Then I'd get to the next step and the next endless round of tutorials and mistakes.

After many visits to CoRo, I had only a few inches of the Agnete Cardigan's collar band done. Literal inches. I had a piece of the one-inch-wide collar a few inches long.

For that amount of effort and hours, I could have had half an easy-knitting sweater already done. Easy knitting is like touch typing. Your brain can stop paying attention and let your hands do their thing. With harder knitting, I still need to look at the knots I'm making.

In the cozy lighting of CoRo, I couldn't easily see the tiny, tiny knots and was tired of watching tutorial videos on a tiny phone screen. At home, I could at least watch the videos on my sixteen-inch laptop, but the lighting wasn't much better than the coffee shop. Berkeley is surprisingly overcast and rainy. Our house's lights were dim.

At home I tried knitting with my camping headlamp, but sitting on my Debbie-approved pile of yoga accessories, I had to put my head too much at a downward angle to fully utilize the light. The headlamp position hurt my neck.

I did some research on Wirecutter and bought an old lady neck-flashlight thing from Amazon. It rests around your neck with a light coming off each shoulder. Each arm of the light is adjustable in its position and brightness. It's marketed for reading in bed but is super popular with older ladies doing fiber crafts. Weavers, knitters, quilters, hand sewists, machine sewists, and others all raved on Amazon about how this allowed them to actually see what they were crafting.

I didn't dare bring my new gadget to the coffee shop, though I doubt the eccentric Berkeleyites would have minded. But, using it at home, it let me see my knitting and easily watch the YouTube tutorials at the same time.

All this improved lighting did not make knitting the cardigan any faster—or the techniques less frustrating. I had to pay attention to every damn stitch.

As Mette had told me, she designs her sweater patterns with a flow state in mind for the knitter. The patterns don't specify which state, but you can guess from the 1-to-5 rating of difficulty. An easy 1 will let your mind wander, perhaps lost in an audiobook. A difficult 5 will require sustained focus, where you'll need to pay close attention to almost every stitch—and maybe use some old lady neck lights.

If you're the type of person for whom a Rubik's Cube puts you in a flow state, you'll probably lean toward sweaters with a difficulty level of 3, 4, or 5. If, instead, you're the person who'd prefer to throw the Rubik's Cube across the room, then you'll probably gravitate toward a 1, 2, or 3. Plus, as we get better, we all change. All of sudden, tiny needles, Fair Isle knitting, or intense techniques might feel relaxing.

In my third trimester, I wanted dreamy. I wanted an easy project. I wanted to knit while zoning out. One of my favorite things to do while knitting is listen to history audiobooks. I was in the middle of *Fallen Glory: The Lives and Deaths of History's Greatest Buildings* by James Crawford and wanted to continue it. Architectural drama, historical context, and lots of interesting facts read to you. What else could you want?

I tried to force the cardigan to be a not-paying-attention knitting flow. I turned on my audiobook and immediately lost my place in the knitting.

It gets cold in Berkeley. I had bought us an indoor temperature reader because I was nervous about how to keep a baby warm in the cold house. It often said 57 degrees Fahrenheit in the morning. It didn't get much higher during the daytime, even on days when the outside temperature was significantly warmer than that.

Our ancient wall heaters only worked if you stood directly in front of them. One, in the living room, clanked along, letting you know it was working really hard—but take two steps away from it and you'd be cold. The other had a fancy automatic turn-off feature that couldn't itself be turned off. It would only run for a few minutes at a time before declaring that the house was in danger of becoming too cozy.

We bought so many electric oil heaters—the kind that gobble up electricity the way Cookie Monster does with gingersnaps. Yes, I knew the 68-to-72 range was slightly arbitrary, that babies have literally lived everywhere in the world. And yet, I worried.

I had a baby being born in the winter. We weren't in the Arctic but still it wasn't comfortable. I wanted to make this little baby feel comfortable, welcomed, and relaxed. I needed to knit him something.

I already had the yarn and pattern for a knitted baby sleep suit that Fiona and I had chosen at Bruun Strik in Copenhagen. All babies in Denmark have these sleep suits. It's a hooded onesie that goes over their clothes so that they're cozy as they sleep outside in their strollers in the winter. Basically, the baby version of tucking into your thick sleeping bag on a cold night while camping—you stay super warm and have the best, deepest sleep.

I hadn't touched that project since getting back from Denmark. But now, the pattern's rating of 3 out of 5 difficulty (easy enough) sounded amazing. I couldn't wait to knit the soft, large yarn on needles that were decently big, but not too big.

I could sit in my supported squat on my pile of Debbie-approved yoga accessories, right next to a cranking oil heater, listen to my audiobook, and knit the softest, squishiest thing. It felt relaxing. I didn't worry about whether the baby would be warm enough or not. I thought about my knitting. I got lost in my audiobook, thinking about faraway and distant past architecture. I felt like I was making a nice welcoming present for the baby—something to make him feel at ease in his new world. I was having fun making something for someone else. I chose to spend time knitting for the baby over my own sweater knitting—and I didn't hate it.

Exploring the Bay Area through its many coffee shops was a way Sam and I could keep wandering around the region without it being too strenuous on my third trimester body. Once at the Blue Bottle in Oakland, Sam was reading a book and I was knitting the baby's sleep suit. Super-wiggly kicks against the wall of my uterus brought me into the immediate moment.

I didn't think too much about it. This tiny baby had been kicking and wiggling inside me almost 24/7. Mostly it was him just bouncing to his own rhythms. Sometimes it was in response to external stimuli. He'd gotten pretty good at orienting his body to nestle against the wall of my uterus.

He clearly loved being held. If I'd press my hand against my belly, he'd maneuver to press his butt, head, foot, or hand into my hand. If I took my hand away before he was ready to be done cuddling, he'd start repeatedly shoving that body part hard into my uterus wall. I'd spend a lot of time like that— in the third trimester position with my hand gently pressed against my belly.

I'd let Sam do the same thing sometimes. He'd put his hand on my belly and gently start talking to the baby. The baby would go bonkers. You could practically hear him shouting *Oh my god, it's Dadddddddddd.* Sam would start talking and the baby would do flips and then nestle intensely into Sam's hand.

But this time at Blue Bottle, the wiggles and kicks would go for about three minutes and then suddenly stop for five or ten minutes, only to restart again for a three-minute-ish period. It was either a full-on dance party or calm nothingness. I suddenly realized: Every time the baby wiggled, ABBA was playing on the coffee shop's playlist. Once it was a different band, the wiggles stopped. Baby loved ABBA.

Later that day, at home, we ran an unscientific study to see what other music the baby liked. Up-tempo, base-forward disco got this baby dancing. The National did not. His favorites included "Dancing Queen" by ABBA, "Stayin' Alive" by the Bee Gees, "Sunny" by Boney M, and "Ring My Bell" by Anita Ward.

I had to stop our Spotify experiment after forty-five minutes because the uterus dance party was starting to be painful.

I kept knitting the baby sleep suit at coffee shops and on my stack of yoga accessories. Slowly I made little sleeves, legs, a body, and the softest little hood. I added some wooden buttons from Denmark, and sewed them on with Japanese green sashiko thread. The thread gave a satisfying pop of color against the neutral beige of the yarn and wood. Playful without being too insistent about it.

For the first time since I had embarked on my creativity quest, I could see some of my wandering efforts coming together. I wasn't bopping between random, seemingly unrelated creative projects. I had sewing and knitting together. Japan and Denmark together—in Berkeley. I was making things out of love for myself and for someone else. It was incredibly satisfying.

I couldn't wait to snuggle this baby, wrap him in this knitted sleep suit, and play him some ABBA. Fiona was right. Sometimes you create things for yourself. Sometimes you do it as an expression of love for someone else. Those two things don't counteract each other. They amplify the creativity and love.

Chapter 12

Cycles

I already knew that creativity didn't need to be original. I had been delighted to realize that I didn't need to reinvent the wheel. I didn't have to be the first to come up with the idea of a sweater or even a specific pattern to follow.

Looking for originality is a fool's errand; we all know this. No one is ever truly the first. Our movies today are all retelling Shakespeare and Jane Austen, who were retelling someone else's stories.

It's the telling of the stories that's fun. I like watching *Bridget Jones's Diary* and *Clueless*, even though I know the plots of *Pride and Prejudice* and *Emma* quite well. It doesn't take away from the swoons and the surprising twists of fate.

Or, as the dancer and choreographer Twyla Tharp wrote in her book *The Creative Habit*, "Someone has done it before?

Honey, it's all been done before. Nothing's really original. Not Homer or Shakespeare and certainly not you. Get over yourself."

We all know this. No one is truly the first. Working with Eli, I relished the instructions of sewing with a pattern. I loved that, in the chaos of everything, I had something where I knew the immediate next step.

I didn't want to let that go—but I also wanted to push things a bit. I always want to push things a bit. I can't help it. I see a limit, a corner, a clearly marked Do Not Enter sign, and wonder what's beyond it. That curiosity helps me get on planes to remote islands and Amazon villages, to jump in the ocean with ama divers, sit at tables with sashiko stitchers, and lounge on couches with knitwear designers.

It also led me to declare in my eighth month of pregnancy that I was going to craft a sweater from sheep to finish. The creativity of Berkeley was soaking in. I wanted to have my hands in the creativity of a sweater beyond the knitting. I still wasn't going for originality or pattern design, but I wanted to touch more of the process. I was curious about shearing the sheep, spinning the yarn, and dyeing the wool.

There's a whole maker's economy catering to these questions. Just like *Bridget Jones's Diary* is *Pride and Prejudice* retold, our current IPO'ed millennials returning to rustic farm life is a retelling of the back-to-land movement of the eighteenth century, the 1920s, the 1970s, and so many other periods when life felt too modern and materialistic. Rustic nature must hold the answers—slowness, manual-ness, and wholeness.

Instead of using Rit Dye, you can buy or gather dried flowers, leaves, barks, insects, nuts, pits, and peels to dye your clothing in your kitchen using your pasta pot. Most local yarn shops sell un-spun wool. How far did I want to take it?

I had this vision of me meeting the millennial sheep-herders and hipster farmers who hope to reinvent our textile system like Alice Waters did for organic food. I'd make a sweater out of local Bay Area yarn—knowing the farmer of the sweater, the same way we imagine we do with our produce bought at farmers' markets.

Then, at the Green Apple Bookstore in San Francisco (where I had previously found Jennifer Banks's *Natality*), I came across Peggy Orenstein's memoir, *Unraveling*. It's got this hardback cover of a slightly out-of-focus sheep staring directly at you against a sky blue background, almost as if you just got knocked off your feet by a sheep getting in your face to ask *What are you doing with my wool?* I couldn't help but pick it up.

After gazing into the sheep's eyes for a tad too long, I read the subtitle, *What I Learned About Life While Shearing Sheep, Dyeing Wool, and Making the World's Ugliest Sweater.* I was delighted to find out that Peggy, who also lived in Berkeley, had done the meet-your-sheep journey I was thinking about.

That evening at home, I devoured her book—maybe this would be a guidebook for me to follow in her footsteps?

I learned that she was already a knitter when 2020 hit: "I couldn't control what was happening in the world, but I could control this: the tossing of the yarn, the tugging of the loop, the counting of the stitches, the accrual of the rows."

So over the course of a year, she set about farm-to-table making her very own sweater. Peggy sheared a sheep, spun the wool, and dyed the yarn with local natural dyes. She created her own sweater design and knit the ugly sweater of the title, a misshapen, color-clashing striped thing. All as a way to deal with the pressures of aging, of her daughter heading to college, and of life anxieties intensified during the COVID pandemic.

"All I knew," Peggy wrote, "was that while everyone else was stress-baking and doomscrolling, I felt an inexplicable, unquenchable urge to confront a large animal while wielding a razor-sharp, juddering clipper; shear off its fleece; and figure out how to make it into a sweater."

Unraveling is a story of time stopped and, of course, forced to continue ever on. During the year of her memoir, Peggy started to untangle metaphorical and real knots in her life. Her father's dementia worsened. She moved to a new house. Biggest of all, Peggy's daughter started college. All along the way, making her "ugly" sweater helped her process these large life knots. "If I've learned nothing else over the last year," she wrote, "it's that 'for now' is all we have. Because life, like a sweater, can come together or unravel: slowly, arduously, oh, so very fast."

I started to wonder: Maybe I would like to know my sheep's name? (Martha is Peggy's sheep.) What if a sweater wasn't just Mette's design, but also Curly Sue's wool? Would that be a more meaningful creative practice?

———

That was all well and good except for the fact that driving an hour north to all the boutique sheep farms sounded terrible. Even worse was the idea of getting out of the car and walking around a farm at eight months pregnant.

Then an email popped into my inbox and solved my quandary. It came from a nearby yarn shop (a six-minute drive) and offered a three-hour workshop on indigo dyeing a sweater's worth of USA-grown yarn. This would be followed by an online knit-a-long hosted by renowned Oakland designer Julie Weisenberger, owner of the mega-popular knitting company Cocoknits. The knit-a-long would knit her "Ruth" pattern—a chunky V-neck with a shawl collar. The indigo leaves were from India but were brewed in the yarn shop's backyard. This, I decided, was good enough to scratch my makers' economy itch—and, practically speaking, might be something I could do before the baby showed up.

The shop, A Verb for Keeping Warm, is a Bay Area establishment co-owned by married business partners Kristine Vejar and Adrienne Rodriguez. Along with their head dyer,

Sarah Ollikkala Jones, they are the go-to experts on naturally dyed yarn.

They opened their Oakland shop in 2012. During the pandemic, they figured out online sales, realizing that they didn't have to keep the store open all the time to still be financially okay. Now their shop hours are 11 to 3 on Saturdays. That's it.

That's how in demand their yarn is. They sell their own hand-dyed yarn and a select few other luxurious brands, including some French hand-dyed brands like La Bien Aimée and Biches & Bûches. All of it is wildly expensive and gorgeous. They dye their yarn in their Oakland shop's backyard, which also doubles as a dye garden. Customers can even special-order the exact dye on specific yarn for their projects.

If a knitter (say, the one writing this book) could manifest their own niche profitable company, I imagine it'd look pretty similar to what Adrienne and Kristine have created for themselves. College sweethearts running a business together that has an extremely enthusiastic fan base across the country who are more than happy to pay their high prices. They make and sell superb products. And they're doing their best to ensure everyone and everything in the supply chain is treated well. Fair wages. Well-tended sheep. Earth-friendly dye. In a very lovely Bay Area way, they're explicit about the intersectionality of what they're trying to change—from how textiles are related to food production, to economic inequality, to global supply chains, to racism, to gender inequity, to everything. It's extremely radical and full of pretty colors in soft textures.

We would be dyeing their "economically accessible" brand, called Bread and Butter. (It's still decently expensive—I spent $120 for five skeins, which is about what I would have paid for Isager yarn. One of their silk yarns, Shimmering Tussah, is dyed with indigo leaves from their backyard and sells for $98 a skein.) The yarn is grown, manufactured, and milled merino wool from farms across the US Mountain West. It comes in two styles—Everyday and Bun. Bun is slightly chunkier. The V-neck called for Everyday.

You can buy Bread and Butter in all the many colors dyed by the shop—or in an undyed white color called Soft Serve if you want to dye it yourself. That's what we'd be using.

What I didn't know going into the dyeing workshop was that Julie, the designer of the pattern we'd knit together, would be there dyeing some yarn herself. Neither did the other workshop attendees. More than one of them let out an accidental yip of excitement and intimidation as they walked into the studio and saw not only Kristine, Adrienne, and Sarah, but also Julie.

Here we were, regular knitters, surrounded by an all-star cast of dyers and designers, there to teach us some of their craft.

After a quick explainer, we all walked out into the rainy, cold backyard and saw giant trash cans under large white tents, the sort you'd see at weddings. The trash cans were full of algae-green liquid that steamed when the lids got lifted off. Indigo dyeing is a kind of alchemy. The dye liquid itself is this bright green, but the minute you pull anything out of the dye, that thing turns a deep blue. Each trash can was tenderly wrapped with a thick wool blanket to keep the dye warm. I, too, was wrapped in wool. I had on a full set of merino long johns under my sweats, wool socks in my sea-foraging boots, a blue apron, and purple kitchen gloves that quickly became blue.

Kristine and Sarah had designed this workshop so that the annoying, hard parts of dyeing were already done before we arrived. As with Eli's sewing workshops, this dyeing workshop let us get down to the most fun parts immediately. We didn't have to brew the indigo, a process that takes days of round-the-clock tending. Like a sourdough starter, a dye bucket of indigo can be reused for a long time, but it requires tending.

Instead of all that work, we got to take our undyed skeins of Everyday yarn and almost immediately could start dipping them into the algae-green liquid. It was three students per dyeing trash can.

We each put two or three skeins of the yarn onto a wooden rod. We then took one rod at a time and rested it on top of the steaming trash cans, letting most of the yarn swim in the dye liquid. After two and a half minutes, we turned the yarn and let the rest soak. Then we took it out, holding the rod in one hand and squeezing the yarn with the other to get some of the liquid out. After this, the yarn rested on a drying rack for ten minutes while someone else took a turn.

You can repeat that cycle as many times as you want. Each time, the yarn will become darker and darker. I did it three times.

When the yarn is pulled out of the dye vat, it's bright green. It turns blue within seconds as it is exposed to oxygen. Indigo dyeing is a ton of chemistry at every single step. The dye liquid's oxygen levels (none) and pH balance (alkaline, between 10 and 11) must be super precise. Plopping the yarn in too fast can mess with the oxygenation, ruining the vat. Instead, you need to slip it in slowly.

A lot of the women at the workshop, including the shop's head dyer, Sarah, had backgrounds in chemistry. As we all oohed and aahed at the beauty of the dyeing process, the conversation quickly turned to: *Why don't they teach chemistry like this to kids in school? This is way better than just memorizing equations.*

It wasn't just the color-changing magic that was giving us a sensory chemistry lesson. Natural indigo dye is known for smelling like poopy diapers, thanks to the fermentation process that removes the oxygen. When the dye batch is new, it doesn't smell that bad. But as more proteins from the wool get added to the batch, it starts to stink. Each dunk of my wool skeins was leaving bits of protein fibers in the liquid, slowly adding to the stink of the vat. A well-done natural indigo dye vat can last a really long time—and stink something horrible.

The poopy diaper smell wasn't the only similarity I was seeing between this dyeing and pregnancy (and eventual motherhood). Both were not polite. They certainly weren't tidy. They were messy and spilled onto everything. And they were permanently transformative, hopefully in good ways.

The green-to-blue magic never got old. Each respective dipping made the blue richer and deeper. We huddled outside in the rain, watching everyone's yarn transform.

We also talked about the sweater this yarn we were dyeing would be knit into. Julie thought that this V-neck sweater she picked for this year's knit-a-long would be perfect for me to use for breastfeeding once the baby showed up. She runs these knit-a-longs every year, emailing super-detailed instructions and how-to videos paced out over a chunk of time—and everyone starts the same sweater at the same-ish time.

I'd never done a knit-a-long before, but many of the workshop attendees had and talked about how they loved the dispersed community feel of doing a project together. Many had gotten into knit-a-longs during the pandemic. All of us talked about how having somewhere (like the backyard we were currently standing in) to do creative things together in person was a real delight.

After we were done dunking the yarn, we needed to rinse the excess dye out and—more chemistry—give it a quick bath in a bucket of water and citric acid to set the color and return its pH back to neutral. Heading toward the washing machine and rinse buckets, I assumed much of the indigo would disappear, leaving the yarn a much lighter color. But barely any did. It really did feel like magic or witchcraft, another practice that is becoming popular within certain feminist millennial cohorts.

I brought my yarn home and let it finish drying on a clothing rack in the garage. The combination of wet wool and natural indigo dye made my yarn stink like a dirty wet dog. After two days, I had dry yarn that smelled delightfully earthy—not poopy—and was ready to be knitted.

I printed out the sweater's instructions and realized I had a problem. Sitting there with my needles and yarn, I came to the horrible realization that I couldn't understand Julie's pattern instructions at all. They included a lot of shorthand notes and her own worksheet method. You'd understand her methods and abbreviations if you've been doing her patterns for a long time. I didn't—it used wildly different techniques and knitting jargon than the Danish patterns. Even though I'm a reasonably confident knitter, I couldn't figure out how to follow her pattern instructions without looking up almost every other word and abbreviation.

There may or may not have been a lot of cursing. I tried to force myself to be positive about it. To find delight in the idea that while knitting has been done for seemingly forever, it can still have such different approaches. In a world that sometimes feels like everything is heading toward increased monopolies and flattened tastes, it is special that you can still have regional and designer variations of something as seemingly straightforward as pattern instructions in the somewhat niche craft of knitting.

Luckily, Julie also had recorded videos. I largely ignored her written pattern instruction and just knit with videoed Julie. It was great. She clearly had made the videos herself over many days as she herself knit the V-neck sweater. She'd make jokes while she was knitting and laugh at her own mistakes.

Julie's patterns are particularly well known for their ability to flatter those with larger breasts. Whereas some patterns just make the overall sweater bigger, Julie shows you how to contour a sweater to your individual body as you're knitting it. Learning directly from video Julie how to do this contouring was great. She uses the same technique (German short rows) that I know to use for making sock heels. I loved learning how to use a technique I already knew from a wildly different application. I felt like a beginner again in the best possible way.

Every and any spare minute was devoted to making this sweater. I was determined that I would have a squishy, soft, dyed-by-me, knit-by-me V-neck sweater to look stylish and cozy in my early postpartum months.

I got the body, the shawl collar, and even almost one arm done. The only problem was that I didn't love how the sweater was turning out. It was a great design, but not for me.

I knew enough about knitting at this point to see how it'd look totally finished. At video Julie's insistence, I even tried on the half-done sweater. It wasn't going to be a sweater I would reach for.

I did something radical, something I'd never done before. I unraveled the sweater. Pulled the needles out of the sweater and started winding the yarn into a ball that turned into two and then three and four balls of yarn. Each knot I'd worked so hard to craft came undone with a satisfying un-looping.

I've certainly abandoned knitting projects before. Projects where the outcome looks suspect, like something I'm not going to wear. Where the design (or my ability to accurately follow instructions) just isn't turning into what I'd hoped it would. Or sometimes it's the color combination I've picked—it looked good in theory but not in the full sweater. (I once tried color blocking, where you do bold color combinations. Neon yellow arms with orange cuffs alongside a navy body sounded good. It looked horrendous.)

With all those projects, I'd left them in a perpetual state of limbo. Not finished, but not undone. There was a lingering sense of potential.

I didn't want to do that with my precious indigo-dyed yarn. I wanted to reuse it for something else that I'd use, not a half-finished sweater or a finished one never worn. I had worked too hard for it. Sure, I hadn't brewed the dye or sheared the sheep. But I had dipped the wool and tended to these specific skeins of yarn. I felt more attached to them than a ball of yarn bought at a shop.

I guess that's the whole point of creating things yourself. You're putting yourself into the process. It's the "you" there that matters in the making. I felt myself in these skeins of yarn. I didn't want to leave this small part of me languishing in a corner of our living room. I wanted to make something of it, something I was proud of and would fondly use. I didn't know yet what that end form would be. But I was pretty certain I could figure it out. Over this creativity research journey, I had gained confidence in my own discernment.

Chapter 13

Delight

Somewhere along the way, I lost the red sock. It's kind of a relief to not know where it is. It means I can cross it off my to-do list without dealing with the pain of quitting something.

But I learned I didn't need to leave projects languishing. I got confidence in unraveling the blue sweater. I still don't know what I will use that yarn for just yet. I get to start again with it. We never really know where we're going anyway.

Babies make that obvious. I gave birth to Finn in mid-February. Those first few weeks were just a Jell-O of panic googling, goofing around with Finn, and playing his to-go lullaby, "Dancing Queen."

Finn loves soft fabric. I wrapped both of us in gentleness during these early weeks. I wore silk and soft sweaters.

Everything was covered in a mess—his and mine. But it didn't matter. We both snuggled in softness.

Some of that softness was store-bought and crafted by other hands in distant factories. I didn't finish any of the sweaters in time to wear them in the early postpartum weeks. So, I bought some. One is made of brown alpaca and is basically a giant blanket posing as a housecoat, wide enough to fit comfortably around both my body and my snuggling baby. Finn loved it so much that sometimes I couldn't feed him while wearing it because he got so distracted. He'd rub his face or the back of his head in the fabric. Try to stick a fistful in his mouth. Utterly delighted in it.

That kind of delight, of course, is why we create. I knew that, in theory, before having my baby. But it became even more apparent after he was born.

The knitted sleep suit was triple the size of tiny newborn Finn. A thick, full-bodied wool suit was way too warm to put on a tiny baby in Berkeley. Plus, despite his love of rubbing his face into soft fabric, he prefers nudity to clothing.

So, it worked out well that the rest of the clothing I created during my pregnancy was for me. It's funny—what you think you want in the future is not often right. You can plan and plan all you want for how you think your kid is going to be raised or for what you think you need (in pregnancy, in parenting, in everyday life). It's only through practice and action that your actual needs reveal themselves.

My sewing was a perfect example of that—the items I was convinced I would absolutely need in early postpartum didn't really end up being useful. The dresses with lots of buttons, the two thick wool coats—these I wore throughout pregnancy but not after Finn showed up. The weather got warmer; PJs replaced the dresses.

The last thing I made in my capsule wardrobe with Eli ended up being the MVP item of my postpartum days—a green teddy fleece French chore jacket with brassy snaps. I wore it so much that the elbows started wearing out. The snaps make for easy adjusting of temperature, a must when, during those first few weeks, my body rapidly switched from too hot to too cold. The pockets are super deep—good for holding an iPhone, headphones, and a bag of trail mix. Perhaps best of all, the green fleece hides spit-up really well and dries quickly after going through the wash.

Before Finn was born, I would have told you that postpartum coziness would come from things I knit myself. Nope. It came from clothing I sewed and from knitted items, like the large alpaca sweater, that I bought. What Finn needed was Sam and me, regardless of what I was wearing (and re-wearing). What I needed was the ability to baby myself in warm, soft delights that let us both feel cozy.

Slowly, over weeks, my creative itch started to come back. When Finn was seven weeks old, I picked up a simple knitting project where all I needed to do was knit stitch after knit stitch. No thinking, just knots. Brain capacity wasn't needed— only rote hand memory. I could start it, knit for a few minutes, and put it down when exhaustion took over or my baby called.

It felt so satisfying to be doing anything creative again. At the same time, this simple act of a few knit stitches here and there was also the absolute maximum of my capacity for many weeks.

As I picked up the knitting, only to put it down again after a few stitches, I thought about the advice that friendly woman had given me at Scrap Night: *When you become a mother, don't stop doing the things that make you you. Don't wait until they're older to get back into creative things. You think it'll only be for a little bit but then you turn around and it's been a decade. Life always gets in the way.*

That advice echoed in my ears in those early days after Finn's arrival. Start living now how you want to live your life. Life doesn't calm down; it just changes. Curveballs keep coming. You can't wait until the time is right. It never is, and it always is.

Putting off what brings me joy is not how I want to live my life—nor, I suspect, is it how Finn would like me to live my life. And yet, in a way that I did not expect while pregnant, I now, as a mother, can hear that siren call with surprising frequency. It sounds like a nap, figuring out the next meal, a laundry load, or scrolling the internet instead of reading. Making sure I get after what brings me joy requires a surprising amount of intentionality and willpower.

Too often, new mothers feel isolated and invisible. You get a lot of attention as a pregnant person, and then the baby shows up and all the attention goes to the baby. You, probably peeing yourself as you sneeze, sleep deprived, feeling emotionally and physically raw, get unintentionally cast aside by your family and friends. *How is the baby?* they ask.

Those who know, though, make sure to check in on you. Ask about how you're doing. Talk about things other than the adorable baby. Check in on your delights and if you're making time to at least think about them. Insist that you're scheduling your own doctor appointments, not just the baby's.

That's important—it can be all too easy to focus on the baby and all that you don't know but are somehow supposed to already know. All three of us learned many seemingly unending new skills in those early days. Some were funny: How to not get peed on during a diaper change with a baby boy? Wipe his belly with a wet wipe a few seconds before you open the diaper. Some were serious: Is he eating enough? How in the world do we know this?

As I panic googled the latest *oh shit, when were we supposed to have learned this?* thing relating to being a parent, I thought again about the term *matrescence*, the process of becoming a mother. I had to look it up again for the details. I relearned that the term is meant to imply that one is always becoming a mother as the child grows, and that it is as awkward/life-altering as a process as is adolescence.

Creative motherhood requires leaning into that matrescence. We all have a need to create—and that can be tricky to do in motherhood. Doing so requires having a support network who gently but insistently remind a pregnant woman or a mother to prioritize things that make her feel vibrant— and demands that others in her life prioritize it. I can't do it alone. My creative practice needs Sam, and it needs our larger community. It needs disco music to soothe my baby. It requires solitude but not aloneness.

That club knows that Hannah Arendt, with her philosophy of birth—natality—was right: The way to live a life is to infuse it with creativity alongside others doing the same. It's a messy abundance that gives us fulfilling lives. There is deep power in birthing, in creating, in new beginnings. It is no wonder that women have so often drifted toward work that lets them engage in creation.

Eventually I started to get bored with the easy knitting. I didn't want to just knit for the sake of it. I wanted a purpose. So I picked up the Sailor Sweater again. It felt great to be knitting for an outcome I cared about and doing it alongside learning how to be a mother.

Writer Kerri ní Dochartaigh is a mother and reflects poetically about being in the world, especially in her memoir *Thin Places*. Having grown up during the Troubles in Derry, Ireland, as child of a Protestant dad and a Catholic mom, she knows a lot about pain and trauma. But she also knows about beauty.

Thin places, a Celtic spiritual term, refers to those physical and metaphorical spaces where the distinction between pain and beauty, past and present, this world and the otherworld, are fragile, porous, and thin. In those early days of mothering, a quote of hers from *Thin Places* often popped into my head: "Time, as we know, like the sea, is a force and a creature all of its own. We can stop neither of them. We stand on the sand, watching as the days become years, as the line made by the tide disappears, as the hungry waves devour the borderline that once defined the land."

Even in the early days, Finn and I loved goofing around with one another. I'd stick out my tongue. He'd stick his tongue out in return and then erupt into proto-laugh sounds.

You could see his little brain and entire body working. He'd wriggle his whole body, flail his arms, and kick his legs. Then the little tongue would come out, and he looked so proud and happy.

I feel the same way doing the hard knitting. I'm wiggly and determined, utilizing seemingly everything in my body to figure out a new knot. Once I get it right, I, too, smile big. The pride and satisfaction are the same. And a gentle reminder to myself to be as soft on myself learning new things as I am on Finn.

I would eventually finish the Sailor Sweater when Finn was almost a year old. I love it: fun stripes, warm, hardy but soft. It taught me that sometimes when you put things aside, you're waiting until you grow into the ability to finish them. You'll come back when you're ready.

It's a similar lesson to the sweater I unraveled. There, I learned that not every project you start is your destiny to finish.

The Agnete Cardigan is still an unknown. I don't yet know if it'll be one of those projects I continually work at—metaphorically wriggling like Finn learning a new skill—or one I know I need to quit. But the confidence I gained with the Sailor Sweater and the decision-making I gained with the V-neck make it worth keeping it around until it's clear which direction to go.

This complicated knitting feels like a metaphor for parenting in many ways. Being sleep-deprived with a newborn, I made mistakes in knitting the Sailor Sweater. Some I undid, but most I left in and continued on.

In life, in parenting, in figuring out creativity in motherhood, in whatever, you will make mistakes. You're creating something. But you need to continue on. You can't freeze with each mistake. If you're looking for perfection, you won't do the thing.

The first few weeks out from Finn's birth, I was pretty sure this book would conclude that while exploring other modes of creativity was interesting, knitting was still my jam—and that, having become a mother, I might just be stuck doing easy knitting forever.

After I started to be able to handle more complicated knitting, I found myself emailing Eli. I needed pants that weren't pajama bottoms and wanted to make them. Together, we sewed some dark teal elastic-waisted flowy pants in cotton twill that still had some structure. Once again, I was sewing for my current body and style.

Then, I found myself googling sea-foraging free-diving spots around the world, wondering if the dissatisfaction I felt with sea foraging in Berkeley had less to do with sea foraging itself. Perhaps, as with the Sailor Sweater, I was putting things aside until I was ready to grow into them? Maybe I just wasn't ready yet.

Or maybe I wasn't approaching it right. I'd been expecting myself to go all-in, like the ama do. I was trying to go grocery shopping in the ocean instead of making sea foraging an occasional adventure. I'm not a full-time ama. But maybe I'm a tourist one. I found some intriguing spots in Ireland, Denmark, Korea, and Indonesia. Someday, I'll have to jump in those oceans, forage, and find out.

I started daydreaming about sewing a wetsuit and perhaps a few more dresses. After all, wasn't that the whole point of this quest? To infuse my life with creativity? Along the way, I realized that I wasn't looking for art, to express a feeling through painting or songs. I wanted creativity I could use. I wanted craft.

I wanted all stages of craft's process, from the excitement that comes from daydreaming about how I would even make a wetsuit to falling down rabbit holes of neoprene thickness and techniques for sewing extremely stretchy material. It's continuing the Sailor Sweater, even when it gets tricky. It's seeing it take shape and realizing that it might be the perfect beach sweater—a wide neck for easily pulling over salty, tangled, wet hair and hardy yarn that would hold up against sand and sun.

I was finally embracing messy middle. The *-ing* in creating.

I thought I was looking for one type of creative modality to scratch an itch. But I didn't find one. I found many that scratched many different types of itches. It turns out I was after increasing the creativity levels throughout my life, not just finding another hobby.

That's the funny thing about being a human—we can't predict ourselves or our needs. All the things I made were way less necessary than just Finn, Sam, and me hanging out. To be even more explicit, none of the things I made were that necessary or important. The only thing that actually matters is us and him—the things make it easier sometimes but can be done without. The spit-up rags. The baby wraps. The pacifiers.

Throughout this creativity exploration, I've been harping on the fact that I needed a creative practice where I ended up with useful things. But what happens when you don't actually need or use those things? I thought all these things I made would be useful—and they somewhat were, but not as useful as I imagined they would be.

Where does that leave creativity as a need? Making things, I found, isn't only about utility. Cozy sweaters and teddy fleece jackets give me some external softness when things feel hard. Like when a little baby is screaming for me to comfort him and I'm just not doing it right. It's those moments where I need to be the adult but also want to be babied myself when a soft sweater can help.

For me, it all came down to that delight. In the form of a thing. In giving my future self a perfect, bespoke present. Along the way in creating that gift, I get my own gift: meditative stillness in the process. My sister is right—every once in a while, it does feel good to do that gift-thinking about someone else that you love.

As the woodworker-writer Peter Korn observes, "None of us enter our studios because the world desperately requires another painting or symphony or chair." He continues, "We engage in the creative process to become more of whom we'd like to be and, just as important, to discover more of whom we might become. We may make things because we enjoy the process, but our underlying intent, inevitably, is self-transformation."

Crafting a creative motherhood feels like getting back into shape. It's a muscle I exercise. I do some knitted rows and then switch back to internet scrolling. I schedule my physical therapy, postpartum Pilates, and slow hikes, knowing that these are the first steps to future days of runs and dives. I figure out how to sew at a machine with a baby strapped onto me (the trick, at least for this baby: good music and frequent walking breaks)—and, more often, sew when Sam tends to Finn.

My favorite Japanese language teacher, Ko, would say halfway through a lesson, "Okay, time to level up!" Then he'd start giving much harder questions for whatever grammar and vocabulary we were learning that day. So when it's something hard, like figuring out how to get a baby to sleep when he's clearly overtired or the million other things you needed to have learned yesterday when parenting, Sam and I laugh and say to each other, "Level up!"

We are ever-changing, always in the process. Making a life is a creative act. In pregnancy I was making a baby. Now, as a mother, I am making myself alongside guiding this little human who is also making himself. If my other creative practices somehow do end up on the back burner in the years to come, I'll do what you do in any sort of "oops" situation: You notice it, level up, and do something about it.

Motherhood is liberating and a joy—that doesn't mean it's not hard. But it's not a bad hard. Running is hard. Learning a language is hard. Creative work is hard. They're all a good hard.

Making beautiful things helps. One day recently, I was washing all of Finn's pacifiers because he had gotten sick with yet another daycare illness. I tossed each washed one onto the kitchen towel on the countertop next to the sink, where some dishes were drying. I realized I was throwing them onto a hanafukin cloth I had sewed with sashiko stitching myself—a lovely wave motif with two tones of blue thread. The dishes drying there included some of my sister's ceramics: handle-less mugs of white porcelain hand-painted with black stripes or triangles.

It was so nice to have tangible things of beauty and care, even on (especially on?) days when everyone had slept terribly. I had a fever. Finn had just vomited. Sam was exhausted. The pacifiers looked so tender among the sashiko and ceramics.

Most days with Finn are not vomit-filled. Most days are giggles, reading, pointing at trees, clapping when he sees a bird fly, long stroller walks, playing music records, and learning how to crawl, sit, stand, and eventually walk. Even more so, it's learning how to fall and get back up.

That's what we're all doing—always getting back up and hopefully playing. Often, when I'd tell a woman about the topic of this book, she'd get excited and tell me all about her creative practices. I discovered that my friends were quilters, woodworkers, jewelry makers, acrylic painters, and almost everything else. These were people I've known well for decades. Acquaintances quickly turned into friends as we discussed creative practices, letting that unfurling conversation help us skip over the purgatory of small talk.

Creativity is everywhere. Women gather at Eli's shop, in cafes around the world, in backyards, and in ama huts to chat, hang out, laugh, cry, and make. These gatherings have existed since seemingly the dawn of humanity and will continue ever onward. To be a woman is to create. The human condition of being born, as Arendt wrote, means that we always have the capacity to begin again. There's tremendous joy and solidarity in the idea of new beginnings and projects always being possible. Creativity provides hope.

Acknowledgments

Elizabeth Hightower Allen: Working with you is an extreme delight. Your edits are deft and your comments kind. Like I said in the last book's acknowledgements: without you, this would be a pile of notes I was pretty sure maybe probably could be a book.

Books are always team efforts. Thank you to graphic designer Cyrus Hernstadt, copy editor Elissa Curcio, and book designer Sarah Lahay for their amazing work on this project.

Fiona: Thank you for being a wonderful little sister and adventure buddy—and for always knowing to bring me extra snacks on said adventures.

Dad: Thanks for driving up in a snowstorm to make me a desk outside, in said snowstorm. And for the countless other times you've dropped everything when I've called you up saying, *Hey Dad...*

Mom: Thanks for always making me whatever cake I wanted for my birthday, and for showing me the many ways creativity can exist in a life. I miss you, and I think you'd be proud of this book.

Sophie and Frances: Thank you for being my friends and always down for some silly adventure. I know there are many more in our future...and I can't wait!

Eli Dembele: Thank you for being such a wonderful sewing teacher and friend. What you've created with Studio Sessions is truly amazing. I'm looking forward to many more hangs in Europe and the Bay Area!

Kazue Yoshikawa: Thank you for teaching me sashiko and for spending so much time with me in Kyoto exploring all the crafting nooks.

Nakaseko Mie, Misako Uemura, Kimiyo Hayashi, Rikako Sato, Naoko Sugiyama, Akiko Tanaka and the wonderful staff at the Toba Sea Folk Museum, Ise-Shima Tourism Board, and Ostasu Cafe Sen: Thank you for diving with me, feeding me ama meals, joining me for lunches, and talking with me about the ama lifestyle.

Debbie Lai: Thank you for teaching me how to stand and move about in my pregnant body. And for helping me get moving again after Finn arrived. I'm continually in awe of (and extremely thankful for) your deep well of knowledge!

Susanne Toft: Thank you for teaching me how to knit. It's so lovely that we now get to be neighbors! Your shop always makes me want to knit more sweaters than I have time for, which is a great problem to have.

Marianne Isager and Nels Gaardahll: Thank you for inviting me up to Tversted and for hosting me the week. You've created a delightful space and company.

Anne Ventzel, Mette Wendelboe Okkels, Maja Klovdal, Helga Jona, and Helga Isager: Thank you for letting me hang around, knit, and ask you a million questions.

Heidi Herrmann and Kirk Lombard: Thank you for teaching me about sea foraging in the Bay Area.

Kristine Vejar, Adrienne Rodriguez, Sarah Ollikkala Jones, and Julie Weisenberger: Thank you for creating and running such wonderful companies and classes. A Verb for Keeping Warm and Cocoknits are true treasures.

Thank you to the many, many people who taught me crafts and skills throughout this process—and to the many more who played in creativity alongside me in countless classes, cafes and meetups.

Sam: I love being your partner in all things, big and small. Goofing around with you is the best. I mean, really, what else is there to do in a life?

Finn: You can't read yet. But someday you might find this book tucked on a shelf somewhere. When you do, please know that you are an absolute joy whose existence is a delight. You're the best thing I've ever made.

About the Author

Sarah Austin Casson is an environmental anthropologist, a job that has brought her all over the world. She has worked with farmers, wilderness rangers, policymakers, scientists, and a bunch more people to look at some of our gnarliest problems: climate change, collapsed prehistoric societies, wilderness conservation, and others. She's interested in how we interact with one another and the natural environment, how we conceptualize our worlds, and what it means to exist in the nuances our world demands.

Numerous grants and awards have funded Sarah's work. These include the Yale Law School's Global Justice Fellowship, Tropical Resources Institute Endowment Fellowship, Council on Southeast Asia Studies Research Grant, Carpenter-Sperry Research Fund, Charles Kao Research Fund, and many others. Her writing has been published in many trade and academic locations. Sarah is an associate member of the Society of Environmental Journalists and a Fellow of the International League of Conservation Writers. She studied at Grinnell College (BA Anthropology) and Yale University School of the Environment (MESc).

Her other books include *How to Start Running (and Enjoy It)*, *How to Do Breathwork (And Enjoy It)*, and *Good Nonsense: A Body in Motion and A Mind at Play*.

She's climbed volcanoes, summited mountains, dived deep into the oceans, and traversed jungles. You'll find her eating delicious food in dense cities and goofing around in remote wildernesses.

She can be found online at: SarahAustinCasson.com